哲 學 經 典 選 讀

王志銘、王靈康、徐佐銘、張國一、鄭鈞瑋、蘇富芝 編著

淡江大學出版中心

目 次

序 言

王志銘

---

1. 什麼是哲學？

中文的「哲學」一詞源自日本人對西方語言 philosophy 這一個字的翻譯。最早使用這一個字的人，是哲學史上大名鼎鼎的蘇格拉底。他因為辯才無礙，而累積了許多跟從學習的人，當這些追隨者忍不住讚嘆蘇格拉底真是一位了不起的 sophist（智者）時，他謙虛地拒絕自封為智者，而將希臘文 philos（愛）跟另一個字 sophia（智慧）合在一起，自詡只不過是個「愛好智慧」而還沒擁有智慧的人。至於如何才能得到智慧？蘇格拉底講出了另一句名言：「承認無知是追求智慧的開端。」

一直到今天，從事哲學研究的人仍然尊奉蘇格拉底所確立的目標與方法，稱他為「哲學之父」。

2. 什麼是經典？

我們都聽過人家嘴邊掛著這是文學經典、宗教經典、社會學經典甚至藝術經典等等用語。這些再平常不過的話，裡頭的「經典」兩個字，到底指的是什麼？

每一門學問裡的經典都有一些共同的特性。首先，它們都指向某些前人甚至古代人留下來的作品。其次，這些作品都「經」得起時間的考驗，

之所以經得起考驗，是因為它們都樹立了某種典範，可以當作所有人學習仿效的永恆對象。最後，這些經典的累積都預告了典範不會只有唯一的單件，而是一直源源不絕的被創造出來呈獻給世人。

3. 為什麼要閱讀哲學經典？

我們每個人都會在人生的某個階段陸陸續續思考一些大大小小的問題？大者如：幸福是什麼？我活著到底為了什麼？小者像：為什麼做人要誠實？或者「為什麼要閱讀經典？」尤其是哲學經典？要回應這些問題，您可以直截草率地回答：「簡單啊！活著就是為了活著嘛！幸福就是讓自己活得爽啊！不誠實怎麼跟人交往呢！閱讀經典就是為了講話時可以落幾句嚇嚇別人吧！」

聽到這種回答，我不會笑這人是個草包，但我要指出：這人從未好好地思考，甚至從未學習如何好好地思考，也就是從未仔細閱讀過哲學經典！

能夠被稱為哲學經典的作品，都是出自歷史上那些非常擅長於思考的哲學大師，他（它）們在「思考」的這一條路上，遠遠走在我們的前端，為我們指引著一條或多條可供參考的路徑。沒有這些指引，我們早就迷失在荒煙蔓草之中，找不到一條精神生命的出路。

套用一句古人的話，「學而不思則罔，思而不學則殆」。閱讀經典——尤其是哲學經典，絕不是要在別人面前炫耀學富五車或記住多少經典名言，而是要您除了自己的胡思亂想之外，也去看看別人怎麼思想，尤其是去看看那些經得起歲月淘汰留存下來的典範哲人怎樣思想。

　　但這一步，並不是要我們一味地相信這些典範陳述的內容必定都是顛撲不破的永恆真理，而只是要我們藉由「大師」的教導，學會更好的思考方式與技巧，學會嘗試「站在別人」的角度來思考與批判所有浮現在我們思想面前的所有答案。

　　因此，閱讀哲學經典，重點不在記誦，甚至不是要從中得到什麼疑難問題的終極解答，更重要的是在理解了作者的原意之後，您還能不能針對作者的思想提出一些問題？如果能做到這一步，那麼您就又回到了「自我思考」，但絕非「胡思亂想」，而配稱得上「很有思想」的人！

4. 經典不應侷限於東方或西方

　　當代文明隨著網路的發達與交通的便利，已不可能像以前那樣關起門來自吹自擂。不同地域因歷史、文化與天才等等不同因素，發展出各別面向的思想與方法，這裡面沒有誰對誰錯的問題，最多只有「誰最能提供沃土與養分，好讓我們在這個充滿變數的人生與世界裡，學會自己安身立命，也幫助他人安身立命」的問題。因此閱讀經典最後還必須加上一種期待，期待任何創造性的詮釋，可以在閱讀之後誕生，不管是出於「囫圇吞棗」或「字斟句酌」的閱讀。我們期待這一本選集裡精挑細選出來的篇章，都可以成為您思想火藥庫爆炸的引子，迸發更多精采動人的思想出來。

　　薪盡火傳，個人的生命終究有其大限，思想的發展卻將永無止境……

王志銘

淡江大學通識與核心課程中心 主任

2016/06/01

一、自然哲學的本原與變動（一）

蘇富芝

單元旨要：

立於蒼穹之下，人們對於自然裡的山河風雲電掣之變、日月星辰周行之動與鳥獸草木之奇，莫不感到驚異而欲一探究竟，其目的則意欲安頓自身的存在。這在驚異當中進行探究的活動，在古代的希臘，則先後分別出現詩人所吟唱的神話以及哲學家所提出的哲學觀點，這意味著：一方面，神話與哲學探問相同的問題：宇宙存在的起源；但另一方面，後於神話出現的哲學，標誌著人們以一種迥異於神話詩人的態度思考這個世界，以不同於神話的方法提出自己的回答，而這些人是最早的自然哲學家。

然而，這批最早的自然哲學家並不是憑空出現的，他們在某種程度上與較早的神話詩人享有以下三個共同的特徵：1. 關注宇宙的開端、結構與運作的原理；2. 認為宇宙是有秩序的，且能被人所理解；3. 宇宙是由神所引導。詩人欲藉由一套一連串前後一致的神話故事，想要從世界的開端，來系統化諸神的生成，以解釋整個世界的起源與生成，並在諸神最高王權的保障之下，世界的秩序得以穩固。詩人的這個嘗試是一種試圖以「理性的一致性」所作的關於「原因」的思考。

這樣的思考乃為自然哲學家所繼承，但是他們拒絕以神話傳統來作為思考的依據，因為神話所講述的這個世界，雖指出自然裡的各種現象與力

量透過諸神們的個人意志而獲得秩序，並由最高王權來保障，但是諸神的任性與一時興起的干預 [1] 不僅為混亂無序留下空間，也並不合乎理性的解釋。因此，自然哲學家丟棄神話傳統來作為解釋世界的依據，試圖以「合乎理性的一致性所作的批判性思考」來提供立論的基礎，在此情況下，自然哲學家對於宇宙源起的原因與原理所提出的解釋，乃主要在以下兩點與神話詩人有別：1. 內在性：這宇宙的秩序本性上是屬於宇宙自身，是源自其內部，而不再是諸神意志干預的結果。宇宙自身內部的原理便足以解釋自身的開端、結構與運作，並能將這些紛呈的自然現象統合為一有機的整體而為有秩序的。2. 普遍性：自然哲學家用以理解各種現象的原理不僅能解釋這些現象為何如此，且能夠恆常地保證這些現象的發生，例如，閃電不再是起因於 Zeus 的意志，而是源自某自然原理，這意味，每當此自然原理出現便會有閃電的發生，這指出，此自然原理不僅解釋了閃電的起因，也作為閃電發生的保證者，在這樣的情況下，諸神一時興起的意志便無立足的空間。

那麼，自然哲學家究竟說了什麼？在這以 Thales 這位最早的自然哲學家為例。當 Thales 說出「宇宙萬有的本原是水」、「地球浮在水上」以及「萬有充滿了神」時，這到底是什麼意思？這與神話的差別到底在哪？在了解 Thales 的意思之前，首先，有兩個名詞必須先弄清楚：1. 宇宙或自然 (nature, *phusis*)，這詞起自於動詞「生長」(to grow) 之意，意指凡是具有生命、能成長、運動的存有者，這也意味，自然存有者本身即內含使之生長的 nature；2. 本原或原理 (principle, *arche*)，這詞的動詞是指「開啟、統治」(to begin, to govern) 的意思，名詞也就是指「開端或起源，也作為具

---

[1] 例如，雷電雲雨是 Zeus 所管，而諸神雖喜愛人們努力工作，但有時會因 Zeus 那無法被猜透的意志，竟使得懶惰的人也能與勤勞的人一樣擁有豐厚的收穫 (*Works and Days,* lines 479-490.)。

有統治意義的『原理』之意」。那麼，探究自然的本原也就是想了解那使自然萬有充滿生命力量的原理到底是什麼，而這原理本身即內於自然存有者裡面作為它們的 nature。

照這樣看來，當 Thales 因觀察到自然萬有從溼潤當中獲得滋養、生長，且溼潤來自於具有能動性的水時，他即推斷水本身可作為使自然萬有充滿生命力量的原理，而提出「宇宙萬有的本原是水」這主張，再加上，由於作為生命的本原本身即是指不朽，而不朽是神的特徵，所以「萬有充滿了神」也就是自然的推論結果。所以當 Thales 因前述的主張而試圖告訴我們，地震的發生不是因為海神 Poseidon 發怒，而是因為地球浮在水上——當地底下的水在運動時，便引起了地震。Thales 對這些觀點所做的思考正是哲學與神話分道揚鑣的關鍵。

文本：

1. Hesiod, Works and Days, lines 42-105[2]

PANDORA AND THE JAR

For the gods keep hidden from men the means of life. Else you would easily do work enough in a day to supply you for a full year even without working; soon would you put away your rudder over the smoke, and the fields worked by ox and sturdy mule would run to waste. But Zeus in the anger of his heart hid it, because Prometheus the crafty deceived him; therefore he planned sorrow and mischief against men. He hid fire; but that the noble son of Iapetus stole again for men from Zeus the counsellor in a hollow fennel-stalk, so that Zeus who delights in thunder did not see it. But afterwards Zeus who gathers the clouds said to him in anger: `Son of Iapetus, surpassing all in cunning, you are glad that you have outwitted me and stolen fire -- a great plague to you yourself and to men that shall be. But I will give men as the price for fire an evil thing in which they may all be glad of heart while they embrace their own destruction.' So said the father of men and gods, and laughed aloud. And he bade famous Hephaestus make haste and mix earth with water and to put in it the voice and strength of human kind, and fashion a sweet, lovely maiden-shape, like to the immortal goddesses in face; and Athene to teach her needlework and the weaving of the varied web; and golden Aphrodite to shed grace upon her head and cruel longing and cares that weary the limbs. And he charged Hermes the guide, the Slayer of Argus, to put in her a shameless mind and a deceitful nature. So he ordered. And they obeyed the lord Zeus the son of Cronos. Forthwith the

---

[2] Trans. by Hugh G. Evelyn-White, *Loeb Classical Library*, No. 57, vol. 1, Harvard University Press, 1914.

famous Lame God moulded clay in the likeness of a modest maid, as the son of Cronos purposed. And the goddess bright-eyed Athene girded and clothed her, and the divine Graces and queenly Persuasion put necklaces of gold upon her, and the rich-haired Hours crowned her head with spring flowers. And Pallas Athene bedecked her form with all manners of finery. Also the Guide, the Slayer of Argus, contrived within her lies and crafty words and a deceitful nature at the will of loud thundering Zeus, and the Herald of the gods put speech in her. And he called this woman Pandora (All Endowed), because all they who dwelt on Olympus gave each a gift, a plague to men who eat bread. But when he had finished the sheer, hopeless snare, the Father sent glorious Argus-Slayer, the swift messenger of the gods, to take it to Epimetheus as a gift. And Epimetheus did not think on what Prometheus had said to him, bidding him never take a gift of Olympian Zeus, but to send it back for fear it might prove to be something harmful to men. But he took the gift, and afterwards, when the evil thing was already his, he understood. For ere this the tribes of men lived on earth remote and free from ills and hard toil and heavy sickness which bring the Fates upon men; for in misery men grow old quickly. But the woman took off the great lid of the jar with her hands and scattered all these and her thought caused sorrow and mischief to men. Only Hope remained there in an unbreakable home within under the rim of the great jar, and did not fly out at the door; for ere that, the lid of the jar stopped her, by the will of Aegis-holding Zeus who gathers the clouds. But the rest, countless plagues, wander amongst men; for earth is full of evils and the sea is full. Of themselves diseases come upon men continually by day and by night, bringing mischief to mortals silently; for wise Zeus took away speech from them. So is there no way to escape the will of Zeus.

2. Hesiod, Theogony, lines 116-147[3]

THE COSMOGONY

In truth at first Chaos came to be, but next wide-bosomed Earth, the ever-sure foundation of all the deathless ones who hold the peaks of snowy Olympus, and dim Tartarus in the depth of the wide-pathed Earth, and Eros (Love), fairest among the deathless gods, who unnerves the limbs and overcomes the mind and wise counsels of all gods and all men within them. From Chaos came forth Erebus and black Night; but of Night were born Aether and Day, whom she conceived and bore from union in love with Erebus. And Earth first bore starry Heaven, equal to herself, to cover her on every side, and to be an ever-sure abiding-place for the blessed gods. And she brought forth long hills, graceful haunts of the goddess Nymphs who dwell amongst the glens of the hills. She bore also the fruitless deep with his raging swell, Pontus, without sweet union of love. But afterwards she lay with Heaven and bore deep-swirling Oceanus, Coeus and Crius and Hyperion and Iapetus, Theia and Rhea, Themis and Mnemosyne and gold-crowned Phoebe and lovely Tethys. After them was born Cronos the wily, youngest and most terrible of her children, and he hated his lusty sire. And again, she bore the Cyclopes, overbearing in spirit, Brontes, and Steropes and stubborn-hearted Arges, who gave Zeus the thunder and made the thunderbolt: in all else they were like the gods, [145] but one eye only was set in the midst of their foreheads. And they were surnamed Cyclopes (Orb-eyed) because one orbed eye was set in their foreheads. Strength and might and craft were in their works.

---

[3] Trans. by Hugh G. Evelyn-White, *Loeb Classical Library*, No. 57, vol. 1, Harvard University Press, 1914.

3. *Thales of Miletus*[4]

(1) DK11 A12--- Ar. Met. A, 3. 983 b 21 f.

The earth floats on the water.

Water is the material cause of all things.

(2) DK11 A22

All things are full of gods. The magnet is alive; for it has the power of moving iron.

(3) DK11 B3

The much-discussed four substances—of which we say the chief is Water, making it as it were the one Element—by combination and solidification and coagulation of the substances in the universe mingle with one another. In what way, I have already explained in Book One.

---

[4] 斷簡 A
Burnet, J., *Early Greek Philosophy*, 3rd edition, University of California Libraries, 1920.
斷簡 B
Freeman, K., *Ancilla to the Pre-Socratic Philosophers*, Harvard University Press, 1948.

4. Anaximander of Mileltus[5]

(1) DK12 A9

Anaximander of Miletos, son of Praxiades, a fellow-citizen and associate of Thales, said that the material cause and first element of things was the Infinite, he being the first to introduce this name for the material cause. He says it is neither water nor any other of the so-called elements, but a substance different from them, which is infinite, from which arise all the heavens and the worlds within them. And into that from which things take their rise they pass away once more, "as is ordained; for they make reparation and satisfaction to one another for their injustice according to the appointed time," as he says in these somewhat poetical terms.

(2) DK12 A11

He says that this is eternal and ageless, and that it encompasses all the worlds.

…And besides this, there was an eternal motion, in which was brought about the origin of the worlds.

---

[5] 斷簡 A

Burnet, J., *Early Greek Philosophy*, 3rd edition, University of California Libraries, 1920.
斷簡 B
Freeman, K., *Ancilla to the Pre-Socratic Philosophers*, Harvard University Press, 1948.

(3) DK12 A16

Further, there cannot be a single, simple body which is infinite, either, as some hold, one distinct from the elements, which they then derive from it, nor without this qualification. For there are some who make this (i.e. a body distinct from the elements) the infinite, and not air or water, in order that the other things may not be destroyed by their infinity. They are in opposition one to another—air is cold, water moist, and fire hot—and therefore, if any one of them were infinite, the rest would have ceased to be by this time. Accordingly they say that is infinite is something other than the elements, and from it the element arise.

(4) DK12 B1

The Non-Limited is the original material of existing things; further, the source from which existing things derive their existence is also that to which they return at their destruction, according to necessity; for they give justice and make reparation to one another for their injustice, according to the arrangement of Time.

(5) DK12 B2

This (essential nature, whatever it is, of the Non-Limited) is everlasting and ageless.

(6) DK12 B3

(The Non-Limited) is immortal and indestructible.

5. Anaximenes of Miletus[6]

(1) DK13 A5

Anaximenes of Miletos, son of Eurystratos, who had been an associate of Anaximander, said, like him, that the underlying substance was one and infinite. He did not, however, say it was indeterminate, like Anaximander, but determinate; for he said it was Air. It differs in different substances in virtue of its rarefaction and condensation.

(2) DK13 A7

From it, he said, the things that are, and have been, and shall be, the gods and things divine, took their rise, while other things come from its offspring. And the form of the air is as follows. Where it is most even, it is invisible to our sight; but cold and heat, moisture and motion, make it visible. It is always in motion; for, if it were not, it would not change so much as it does. When it is dilated so as to be rarer, it becomes fire; while winds, on the other hand, are condensed Air. Cloud is formed from Air by felting; and this, still further condensed, becomes water. Water, condensed still more, turns to earth; and when condensed as much as it can be, to stones.

---

[6] Burnet, J., *Early Greek Philosophy*, 3rd edition, University of California Libraries, 1920.

問題討論：

1. Prometheus 與 Pandora 的故事如何解釋人的存在？

2. 神話詩人與自然哲學家如何解釋「神」(the divine) 這概念？

3. 怎麼理解 Anaximander 所提出的 Unlimited(APERION)？

延伸閱讀：

1. Barnes, J., *Early Greek Philosophy*, Harmondsworth, 1987.

2. Cornford, F. M., *From Religion to Philosophy*, London, 1912.

3. Vernant, J.-P., *Myth and Thought among the Greeks*, London, 1983.

二、自然哲學的本原與變動（二）

蘇富芝

單元旨要：

　　自然哲學家對本原的探究引出另外兩個主要被關注的問題：第一，本原與其所解釋的這些生滅變動的現象之間的關係為何？而哲學家在這探究當中則進一步反思到：作為探究者的我們，究竟是以什麼樣的方式來認知，而所認知的是否真是所探求的智慧，以及這樣的本原智慧是否真能為人所獲得……等知識論的問題；第二，原本主宰天上人間秩序與正義的傳統諸神，在被自然哲學家抹去後，留下一個亟待重新定義的空間，這不僅關乎如何理解那具有神性的萬有本原，也關乎如何理解人間的道德秩序及其根源。以下，我們將分別從這兩位哲學家 (Xenophanes of Colophon 與 Heraclitus of Ephesus) 的觀點來理解上述問題。雖然，由於他們的研究興趣使然，使其側重的面向有所不同，但至少能為我們提供一個總體的理解藍圖。

1. Xenophanes of Colophon

(1) 批判傳統諸神，建立關於「神」的新觀點

　　首位對傳統諸神提出猛烈批判的 Xenophanes，以下列五個面向提出他的批評：(a) 傳統諸神的不道德行為 (DK21 B11) 是不恰當的；(b) 神

人同形同性；若牛、馬也能塑造自己的神，想必也是如同牛、馬一般 (DK21 B15)；(c) 傳統諸神是被生出來的；若如此，這似乎否定神的永生 (DK21 A12)；(d) 神有位階；說「神擁有統治祂的主人」，這似乎是不虔敬的 (DK21 A32)；(e) 神到處忙碌插手人間事務，對神來說並不恰當，靜止於一處才是適合神的 (DK21 B26)。這些批評則從另一個面向指出關於「神」的正確看法：神是善的，不是人模人樣的，是永恆的，自足的，靜止的。Xenophanes 以什麼作為批判的標準？以「恰當、合適」(epiprepei, it is fitting)[1]。Xenophanes 的這個「恰當、合適」的評判準則影響深遠，不僅悲劇詩人如 Euripides 引用，後代的哲學家如 Plato、Stoics 也引用，並且 Stoics 還新鑄一個字「theoprepes」(that which befits the divine nature) 以使用在神學的範疇上。在這準則下，Xenophanes 還提出「神是一」(DK21 B23) 以與傳統多神論對抗，另外還指出，神對於這個世界的作用方式為「不費任何吹灰之力，藉由心靈的思考，而啟動萬有」(DK21 B25)，一方面這也許是因為神是靜止不動，另一方面也許是要指出神是以思考來統治世界，而不是像傳統諸神那樣憑著一時興起。另外，還有一個問題是，Xenophanes 對於神與世界之間的關係並沒有清楚說明：這個世界充滿變動，而如果神是靜止的，那神便無法是這世界的一部分；另，神若是靜止於一處，但又要啟動萬有，那麼，神就必須無處不在，但這又與神靜止於一處矛盾。

---

[1] 這字源自「對和諧均衡的感受」，這種感受不僅出現在古希臘的藝術家及其作品上，也在政治學與倫理學的領域有重要地位。Jaeger, W. W., *The Theology of the Early Greek Philosophers*, pp. 49-50.

(2) 作為人類德性的哲學智慧

　　Xenophanes 指出，人的德性 (*arete, perfectness*) 並不是要在運動會上拿桂冠，而是要以獲得哲學智慧為目的，哲學智慧除了對神有正確認識並以高雅公正的話語讚美神之外，更要以城邦的正義秩序與福祉為目的 (DK21 B1-2)。 哲學智慧對人類的這個重要貢獻於 Xenophanes 詩歌裡首度出現。

(3) 質疑人類獲得真理的可能性

　　第一位反思並質疑人類能否獲得真理的是 Xenophanes。在關於神及其相關的事情上，Xenophanes 認為沒有人能獲得關於祂們的「知識」，可能最多只有如同他自己所陳述的那些「與真理相似的信念」(DK21 B34-35)；另一方面，Xenophanes 並不認為有「天啟」可作為知識的來源，而是，對人們來說，人們可獲得的乃是以長期辛勞的研究所逐步發現到的更好的觀點 (DK21 B18)。

　　Xenophanes 以上三項論點都對之後的哲學活動產生深遠影響，並反轉自然哲學往後的研究對象：從對自然萬有的研究轉移至對此研究的反思並試圖提供更穩固的基礎。

2. Heraclitus of Ephesus

(1) 萬有的本原——Logos

　　如同 Xenophanes (DK21 A30)，Heraclitus 也認為宇宙是永恆的 (DK22 B30)，所以只需解釋宇宙的秩序如何維護，無須說明宇宙怎麼出現的。Heraclitus 提出 Logos 這個本原來說明所有一切變動，以「一」與「多」

這組對立者來表達，以指出：多中有一，一中有多 (out of all things there comes a unity, and out a unity all things) (DK22 A10)；且 Heraclitus 以「一切的對立」（例如冷熱、乾溼、年輕與老年……等等）來代表「多」，因為若極端的對立者都能得到解釋，更何況其他？！Heraclitus 以弓為例：弓臂與弓弦必須處在同等張力下的對立方向，唯有弓臂與弓弦彼此對立，才能成就一把完整的弓並發揮弓的功能；從另一方面來說，一把要能發揮功能的弓必須要有這種彼此對立的弓臂與弓弦。這種「對立中的統一」說明了 Logos 與宇宙的變動現象之間的關係：和諧與秩序來自於對立者之間的爭鬥，爭鬥當中體現了 Logos 的法則，也被稱為正義 (DK22 A8, 80)。

(2) 道德秩序植根於自然秩序

Heraclitus 是第一位將人類的道德智慧賦予哲學基礎的哲學家。他認為，一個有道德智慧的人是能理解萬有的本原──Logos，因為這個 Logos 正作為人們行動與言說的根據 (DK22 B1)，而擁有正確思考與行動，正是所有人所最應努力獲得的德性 (DK22 B112)；另一方面，這個 Logos 還是所有人所應奮力獲得的神聖法律 (DK22 B44)，因為所有人間城邦的法律都根植於此 (DK22 B114)。

(3) 如何獲得哲學智慧

相較於有智慧的人來說，Heraclitus 認為大多數無知的人都處在睡覺的狀態，因為他們即使面對著 Logos 也不認識 (DK22 B17)，那麼，睡著的人如何醒來？Heraclitus 認為唯有往自己內心深處探索 (DK22 B101) 並能正確解讀感官知覺所提供的訊息（參見 DK22 B107），如此才能獲得真正的智慧，亦即於宇宙整體當中了解各個部分之間的關係 (DK22 B41)。

文本：

1. Xenophanes of Colophon[2]

(1) DK21 B1, lines 21-24

Let him not sing of Titans and Giants—those fictions of the men of old—nor of turbulent civil broils in which is no good thing at all; but to give heedful reverence to the gods is ever good.

(2) DK21 B11

Homer and Hesiod have ascribed to the gods all things that are a shame and a disgrace among mortals, stealings and adulteries and deceivings of one another.

(3) DK21 B14

But mortals deem that the gods are begotten as they are, and have clothes like theirs, and voice and form.

(4) DK21 B15

Yes, and if oxen and horses or lions had hands, and could paint with their hands, and produce works of art as men do, horses would paint the forms of the gods like horses, and oxen like oxen, and make their bodies in the image of their several kinds.

---

[2] Burnet, J., *Early Greek Philosophy*, 3rd edition, University of California Libraries, 1920.

(5) DK21 B16

The Ethiopians make their gods black and snub-nosed; the Thracians say theirs have blue eyes and red hair.

(6) DK21 B18

The gods have not revealed all things to men from the beginning, but by seeking they find in time what is better.

(7) DK21 B23

One god, the greatest among gods and men, neither in form like unto mortals nor in thought . . . .

(8) DK21 B24

He sees all over, thinks all over, and hears all over.

(9) DK21 B25

But without toil he swayeth all things by the thought of his mind.

(10) DK21 B26

And he abideth ever in the selfsame place, moving not at all; nor doth it befit him to go about now hither now thither.

(11) DK21 B34

There never was nor will be a man who has certain knowledge about the gods and about all the things I speak of. Even if he should chance to say the complete truth, yet he himself knows not that it is so. But all may have their fancy.

(12) DK21 B35

Let these be taken as fancies something like the truth.

2. Heraclitus of Ephesus[3]

(1) DK22 B1

Though this Word is true evermore, yet men are as unable to understand it when they hear it for the first time as before they have heard it at all. For, though, all things come to pass in accordance with this Word, men seem as if they had no experience of them, when they make trial of words and deeds such as I set forth, dividing each thing according to its nature and showing how it truly is. But other men know not what they are doing when awake, even as they forget what they do in sleep.

(2) DK22 B2

Though wisdom is common, yet the many live as if they had a wisdom of their own.

---

[3] Burnet, J., *Early Greek Philosophy*, 3rd edition, University of California Libraries, 1920.

(3) DK22 B8

It is what opposes that helps.

(4) DK22 B10

Couples are things whole and not whole, what is drawn together and what is drawn asunder, the harmonious and discordant. The one is made up of all things, and all things issue from the one.

(5) DK22 B12

You cannot step twice into the same rivers; for fresh waters are flowing in upon you.

(6) DK22 B30

This world, which is the same for all, no one of gods or men has made; but it was ever, is now and ever shall be an ever-living fire, with measures kindling and measures going out.

(7) DK22 B49a

We step and do not step into the same rivers; we are and are not.

(8) DK22 B50

It is wise to hearken, not to me, but to my Word, and to confess that all things are one.

(9) DK22 B60

The way up and the way down is one and the same.

(10) DK22 B61

The sea is the purest and the impurest water. Fish can drink it, and it is good for them; to men it is undrinkable and destructive.

(11) DK22 B80

We must know that war is common to all and strife is justice, and that all things come into being and pass away (?) through strife.

(12) DK22 B86

(The wise man) is not known because of men's want of belief.

(13) DK22 B89

The waking have one common world, but the sleeping turn aside each into a world of his own.

(14) DK22 B101

I dived into myself.

(15) DK22 B102

To a god all things are fair and good and right, but men hold some things wrong and some right.

(16) DK22 B107

Eyes and ears are bad witnesses to men, if they have souls that understand not their language.

(17) DK22 B112

Self-control is the highest virtue, and wisdom is to speak truth and consciously to act according to nature.

(18) DK22 B113

Thought is common to all.

(19) DK22 B114

Those who speak with understanding must hold fast to what is common to all as a city holds to its law, and even more strongly. For all human laws are fed by the one divine law. It prevails as much as it will, and suffices for all things with something to spare.

(20) DK22 B116

All men are have the capacity to come to know themselves and to (have/be) self-control.

(21) DK22 B119

Man's character is his fate.

(22) DK22 B123

Nature loves to hide.

問題討論：

1. 如何理解 Heraclitus 的「對立中的統一」？

2. 怎麼解釋 Xenophanes 在宗教上的革新？

3. 你會如何以 Xenophanes 的思考方式來看待現代社會裡的各種宗教，試舉例？

延伸閱讀：

1. Freeman, K., *Companion to the Pre-Socratic Philosophers*, Oxford, 1946.

2. Jaeger, W. W., *The Theology of the Early Greek Philosophers*, Oxford, 1947.

3. Kirk, G. S., and Raven, J. E., *The Presocratic Philosophers*, Cambridge, 1957.

三、古希臘的智者學派

蘇富芝

單元旨要：

西元前 5 世紀中葉左右，一群自稱能教導「德性—善」(arete-agathos, excellence-good) 的教師穿梭於古希臘各個城邦進行收費講學的活動，他們被稱為智者 (Sophists)。智者認為經由他們的教導能幫助人們在私人及公眾生活裡取得成功，成為一個具有德性—善的人。這個主題（德性與善）原本即是古希臘文化裡對「人」所進行的探問核心：怎樣才是一個最好的人？如何成為這樣的人？（What's the best kind of person to be? And how?）最早，在荷馬史詩時期，所重視的「德性—善」是那能在戰場裡發揮殺敵取勝的英雄理想 (the heroic ideal)，亦即具有高貴出生、俊美、勇敢、富有、虔誠、有謀略、具領導力……等等德性集於一身的個人英雄主義式的戰士理想，與其所對應的社會條件則是以農業經濟為主的貴族政體。然而之後隨著經濟與政治情勢的改變，頻繁的貿易活動促使中產階級大量興起，經濟結構的轉變導致社會貧富差距擴大，因此要求政治改革的力量湧現，於此，貴族政體崩解，一股還政於民的政治力量促成了民主政體的興起。

在這樣的民主新時代裡，荷馬式的英雄理想開始褪色，新的「德性—善」範型則還在摸索，此時，新建立的直接民主政體使得每位公民都有權利也有義務參與政治事務，都可在公民大會裡論說自己的政治主張來試圖影響說服他人。在這樣的情況下，出現了智者。他們宣稱能透過所教導的演說術以及

各種類型的知識（包括自然哲學）來幫助人們培養政治德性，以在公民大會、法庭上或其他場合裡提出有力的論說來說服他人，以此獲得權力、名聲與金錢，而這就是人生的成功，就是最好的人。這就是智者為「德性—善」所提出的新範型。

然而，智者的教導面臨兩項批評：1. 販賣「德性—善」：對古希臘人來說，傳統的「德性—善」是必須從小由家庭開始經過各個階段的培育長久薰習而成，這種教養實在是很難能用金錢交易而獲得；2. 詭辯的演說術：不論在公民大會、法庭或其他場合，演說術的目的是要在論辯中取勝以達到說服他人的效果，而智者認為若能針對同一個對象進行正面與反面的論說，例如對同一件事既稱正義又稱不正義、對同一個人既稱讚又責備，那便具有「將弱的論證轉為強的論證」的詭辯能力（參見 DK80 A21），而能在論辯當中無往不勝。但是，這種只為取勝的論辯實際上並不在乎所談的是否是真理，而是只在乎所說的是否為人所相信。智者認為那些在法庭或議會裡準備做決定的法官、陪審員或公民們都是依據各方所提出的論說來進行判斷，因此，要緊的是這些論說是否具有說服力而能令人信服，至於真相到底為何其實並不重要，因為在那做決斷的並不是真理，而是那些掌握決定權的人們。

這樣的想法被著名的智者 Protagoras 表達如下：「人為萬有的尺度—是即如是，不是即如不是。」(A human being is the measure of all things—of things that are, that they are, and of things that are not, that they are not.) (DK80 B1) 這指出，真理並不擁有獨立於覺知者（或思考者）的客觀存在，而是存在於覺知者（或思考者）。例如，同一陣風吹過來，A 感到冷，B 感到熱，這陣風之為冷風或熱風取決於 A（或 B）所認為的：若 A「認為」某某如此，那麼，某某「實際」即為如此。

Protagoras 這觀點其實蘊含當時哲學思考的核心主題「NOMOS-PHYSIS」，前者是指「習俗與法律」(convention, customs and laws)，其本意為「人們所認為（對）的」(what people believe; what's believed to be right)，而這具有變動性，因為 NOMOS 會隨著那在不同地域與時間當中的人們的想法而改變，後者則指「天生而有的本性，或真實」(the essential nature or the reality)，這是恆常的且具有必然性。這個 NOMOS-PHYSIS 的主題則來自當時的自然哲學家的研究成果—在「現象」與「真實」(APPEARANCE-NATURE) 之間的明確區別，而這尤其展現在原子論者的立場上：他們認為，無數微小不可分、不可被知覺的原子在虛空裡的運動乃是整個宇宙的真相，而所有呈現在感官知覺面前的這些味道、顏色、聲音……等等實際上是從覺知者與被覺知者的原子之間的運動所產生的，它們其實並沒有自己真正的存在，在這樣的情況下，感覺的存在是相對於覺知者來說的並被覺知者認為 (by convention) 是甜的、苦的、熱的、冷的……等等的「現象」，然而這些現象實際上並不存在，真正存在的只有這獨立於覺知者的客觀存在：原子在虛空裡的運動（參見 DK68 B9），亦即「真實」。

原子論者的論點在知識論與倫理學方面引發議論。1. 知識論方面：由於感覺呈現的現象實際上並不存在，因此，原子論者否定感覺能為我們帶來任何真理而只能帶來劣等的判斷（參見 DK68 B11），但是，他們又說感覺是探尋真相的踏腳石（參見 DK67 A97），然而，又強調感覺與真理之間的鴻溝（參見 DK68 B6-10），那麼我們是否能獲得關於那不可被知覺到的宇宙真相？這似乎是個疑問並也引發懷疑論。Protagoras 便是在這樣的情況下提出：「人為萬有的尺度—是即如是，不是即如不是。」(DK80 B1) 將「NOMOS-PHYSIS」之間的對立取消，主張 NOMOS 就是 PHYSIS，亦即讓「人們所認為的」等同於「真正存在的」。2. 倫理學方面：原子論者認為，任何事情的發生都不是偶然，而是來自原子依據自身的大小、形狀與位置在虛空裡所做的必然性

運動（參見 DK67 B2），這種必然性運動本身並不具有任何（神聖的）意圖與目的（DK68 A66），只有原子出於機械性的必然所作的強迫性運動（DK67 A16）。這樣的觀點引發一場倫理學上的危機—道德主體的喪失：通常之所以賦予某行為某種意義與目的是因為那是出自選擇與做決定的結果，也就是出於自由意志，在這樣的情況下，具有自由意志的主體成為可擔負起被究責的道德主體，然而，若一切實際上皆只是原子的必然運動而沒有為自由意志留下空間，那麼便不會有道德主體的存在，並連帶地讓道德的存在面臨崩解。

智者們運用了以上當時這些由自然哲學對「APPEARANCE-NATURE」所做的研究以及其中所蘊含的「NOMOS-PHYSIS」的觀點，在民主政體的推波助瀾下，對他們所關心的政治德性裡的法律與道德進行探究，並在以贏得論辯為前提下，智者其精巧的詭辯演說術鬆動了當時的法律與道德的傳統根基，而進一步地在政治、道德與社會各層面引發種種論辯與質疑，他們的觀點雖在思想上造成極大的風潮，但實際上卻引發道德價值崩解的危機，而這最能體現在智者對「德性—善」所提出的新範型：透過金錢交易來培育政治德性，以此獲得權力、名聲與金錢。

對於那當時常因與人對話而顯得與智者一樣智巧的哲學家蘇格拉底來說，他質疑智者所提出的「德性—善」。蘇格拉底要問的是，我們每天汲汲營營地生活，想盡辦法實現目標（亦即我們的德性—善），但是卻從未仔細思考到底這些目標是否真值得我們為之追尋；蘇格拉底要我們反身去思索到底什麼目標才是真正有內在價值的，能讓我們從根源上把握住生命的美與善：「高貴的人啊，你乃身為那以智慧與強盛聞名於世的最大城邦 -- 雅典 -- 的公民。然而，你卻汲汲於追求金錢、名聲與榮譽，而對睿智、真理以及如何使靈魂達至完善等問題卻置若罔聞，難道你不感到慚愧嗎？」(Plato, *Apology of Socrates* 29d-e) 而這正是蘇格拉底哲學的起點。

文本：

1. *Fifth-Century Atomism: Leucippus and Democritus*[1]

(1) DK67 A7

Leukippos and Demokritos have decided about all things practically by the same method and on the same theory, taking as their starting-point what naturally comes first. Some of the ancients had held that the real must necessarily be one and immovable; for, said they, empty space is not real, and motion would be impossible without empty space separated from matter; nor, further, could reality be a many, if there were nothing to separate things. And it makes no difference if any one holds that the All is not continuous, but discrete, with its part in contact (*the Pythagorean view*), instead of holding that reality is many, not one, and that there is empty space. For, if it is divisible at every point there is no one, and therefore no many, and the Whole is empty (*Zeno*); while, if we say it is divisible in one place and not in another, this looks like an arbitrary fiction; for up to what point and for what reason will part of the Whole be in this state and be full, while the rest is discrete? And, on the same grounds, they further say that there can be no motion. In consequence of these reasonings, then, going beyond perception and overlooking it in the belief that we ought to follow the argument, they say that the All is one and immovable (*Parmenides*), and some of them that it is infinite (*Melissos*), for any limit would be bounded by empty space. This, then, is the opinion they expressed about the truth, and these are the reasons which led them to do so. Now, so far as arguments go, this conclusion does seem to follow; but, if we appeal to facts, to hold such a view

---

[1] Burnet, J., *Early Greek Philosophy*, 3rd edition, University of California Libraries, 1920.

looks like madness. No one who is mad is so far out of his senses that fire and ice appear to him to be one; it is only things that are right, and things that appear right from habit, in which madness makes some people see no difference.

Leukippos, however, thought he had a theory which was in harmony with sense, and did not do away with coming into being and passing away, nor motion, nor the multiplicity of things. He conceded this to experience, while he conceded, on the other hand, to those who invented the One that motion was impossible without the void, that the void was not real, and that nothing of what was real was not real. "For," said he, "that which is strictly speaking real is an absolute *plenum*; but the *plenum* is not one. On the contrary, there are an infinite number of them, and they are invisible owing to the smallness of their bulk. They move in the void (for there is a void); and by their coming together they effect coming into being; by their separation, passing away."

(2) DK67 A8

Leukippos of Elea or Miletos (for both accounts are given of him) had associated with Parmenides in philosophy. He did not, however, follow the same path in his explanation of things as Parmenides and Xenophanes did, but, to all appearance, the very opposite (R. P. 185). They made the All one, immovable, uncreated, and finite, and did not even permit us to search for *what is not*; he assumed innumerable and ever-moving elements, namely, the atoms. And he made their forms infinite in number, since there was no reason why they should be of one kind rather than another, and because he saw that there was unceasing becoming and change in things. He held, further, that *what is* is no more real than *what is not*, and that both are alike causes of the things that come into being; for he laid down that the substance of the atoms was compact and full, and he called them *what is*, while they moved in the void which he called *what is not*, but affirmed to be just as real as what is.

2. Protagoras the Sophist[2]

(1) DK80 B1

(*From 'Truth' or Refutatory Arguments'*). Of all things the measure is Man, of the things that are, that they are, and of the things that are not, that they are not.

(2) DK80 B2

(*From 'On Being'*). (Porphyry: '*Few of the writings of Plato's predecessors have survived, otherwise Plato perhaps would have been detected in further plagiarisms. fit any rate, in the place where I happened to have been reading in Protagoras' book "On Being" the argument he uses against those who make Being One, I find that he uses the same refutatory terms. For I took the trouble to memorise the passage word for word*').

(3) DK80 B4

(*From 'On the Gods'*). About the gods, I am not able to know whether they exist or do not exist, nor what they are like in form; for the factors preventing knowledge are many: the obscurity of the subject, and the shortness of human life.

---

[2] Freeman, K., *Ancilla to the Pre-Socratic Philosophers*, Harvard University Press, 1948.

(4) DK80 B6a

(*Protagoras was the first to say that there were two contradictory arguments about everything*).

(5) DK80 B6b

To make the weaker cause the stronger.

(6) DK80 B8

(Plato, *Sophist* 232D, E: '*Those views regarding all the arts and each art separately, what one must say against the craftsman practising each: views which stand published in writing for all to learn if they wish.—I think you must mean the views of Protagoras on wrestling and the other arts*').

(7) DK80 B12

(*Graeco-Syrian Maxims: Protagoras said*): Toil and work and instruction and education and wisdom are the garland of fame which is woven from the flowers of an eloquent tongue and set on the head of those who love it. Eloquence however is difficult, yet its flowers are rich and ever new, and the audience and those who applaud and the teachers rejoice, and the scholars make progress and fools are vexed—or perhaps they are not even vexed, because they have not sufficient insight.

3. Antiphon the Sophist[3]

DK87 B44

Justice, then, is not to transgress that which is the law of the city in which one is a citizen. A man therefore can best conduct himself in harmony with justice, if when in the company of witnesses he upholds the laws, and when alone without witnesses he upholds the edicts of nature. For the edicts of the laws are imposed artificially, but those of nature are compulsory. And the edicts of the laws are arrived at by consent, not by natural growth, whereas those of nature are not a matter of consent.

So, if the man who transgresses the legal code evades those who have agreed to these edicts, he avoids both disgrace and penalty; otherwise not. But if a man violates against possibility any of the laws which are implanted in nature, even if he evades all men's detection, the ill is no less, and even if all see, it is no greater. For he is not hurt on account of an opinion, but because of truth. The examination of these things is in general for this reason, that the majority of just acts according to law are prescribed contrary to nature. For there is legislation about the eyes, what they must see and what not; and about the ears, what they must hear and what not; and about the tongue, what it must speak and what not; and about the hands, what they must do and what not; and about the feet, where they must go and where not. Now the law's prohibitions are in no way more agreeable to nature and more akin than the law's injunctions. But life belongs to nature, and death too, and life for them is derived from advantages, and death from disadvantages. And the advantages laid down by the laws are chains upon nature, but those laid down by nature are free. So that the things

---

[3] Freeman, K., *Ancilla to the Pre-Socratic Philosophers*, Harvard University Press, 1948.

which hurt, according to true reasoning, do not benefit nature more than those which delight; and things which grieve are not more advantageous than those which please; for things truly advantageous must not really harm, but must benefit. The naturally advantageous things from among these . . .

(*According to law, they are justified*) who having suffered defend themselves and do not themselves begin action; and those who treat their parents well, even though their parents have treated them badly; and those who give the taking of an oath to others and do not themselves swear. Of these provisions, one could find many which are hostile to nature; and there is in them the possibility of suffering more when one could suffer less; and enjoying less when one could enjoy more; and faring ill when one need not. Now if the person who adapted himself to these provisions received support from the laws, and those who did not, but who opposed them, received damage, obedience to the laws would not be without benefit; but as things are, it is obvious that for those who adapt themselves to these things the justice proceeding from law is not strong enough to help, seeing that first of all it allows him who suffers to suffer, and him who does, to do, and does not prevent the sufferer from suffering or the doer from doing. And if the case is brought up for punishment, there is no advantage peculiar to the sufferer rather than to the doer. For the sufferer must convince those who are to inflict the punishment, that he has suffered; and he needs the ability to win his case. And it is open to the doer to deny, by the same means . . . and he can defend himself no less than the accuser can accuse, and persuasion is open to both parties, being a matter of technique. . . .

We revere and honour those born of noble fathers, but those who are not born of noble houses we neither revere nor honour. In this we are, in our relations with one another, like barbarians, since we are all by nature born the same in every way, both barbarians and Hellenes. And it is open to all men to observe the laws of nature, which are compulsory. Similarly all of these things can be acquired by all, and in none of these things is any of us distinguished as barbarian or Hellene. We all breathe into the air through mouth and nostrils, and we all eat with hands. . .

(*From another book of 'Truth'*)

If justice were taken seriously, then witnessing the truth among one another is considered just, and useful no less for men's business affairs. But he who does this is not just, since not to wrong anyone unless wronged oneself is just; for it is inevitable for the witness, even if he witnesses to the truth, nevertheless to wrong another in some way, and at the same time himself be wronged later, because of what he said; in that because of the evidence given by him, the person witnessed against is condemned, and loses either money or his life, through someone to whom he does no wrong. Therein therefore he wrongs the man against whom he gives evidence, in that he wrongs someone who did him no wrong; and he himself is wronged by the man against whom he gave evidence, because he is hated by him for having given truthful evidence. And (*he is wronged*) not only by this hatred, but also because he must for the whole of his life be on his guard against the man against whom he gave evidence; for he has an enemy such that he will say or do him any harm in his power. Indeed, these are clearly no small wrongs which he himself suffers and which he inflicts; for these cannot be just, nor can the demand to do no wrong (*if one is not wronged?*) But it is inevitable that either both are just or both unjust. It is clear, also, that to judge, give judgement, and arbitrate for a settlement are not just; for that which helps some, hurts others; and in this case, those who are benefited are not wronged, but those who are injured are wronged. . . .

問題討論：

1. 你是否同意 Protagoras 的名句「人為萬有的尺度」？為什麼？

2. 請解釋「NOMOS-PHYSIS」。

3. 如何將本單元的理解應用在現今的社會？

延伸閱讀：

1. Guthrie, W. K. C., *In the Beginning: Some Greek Views on the Origins of Life and the Early State of Man*, London, 1957.

2. Jaeger, W. W., *Paideia: The Ideals of Greek Culture*, vol.1, 2nd edition, Oxford, 1945.

3. Kerferd, G. B., *The Sophistic Movement*, Cambridge, 1981.

四、蘇格拉底與柏拉圖（一）

蘇富芝

單元旨要：

　　20 世紀的英國哲學家懷海德 (A. N. Whitehead) 說：整個歐洲哲學傳統皆為柏拉圖哲學的註腳。然而，若要真正了解柏拉圖，則必定要論及他的老師蘇格拉底，因為蘇格拉底正是柏拉圖哲學的起點與核心。西元前 399 年，當時那在柏拉圖眼裡被認為是「在所有活著的人中最為正義的」(Plato, *Letter* VII 324e) 蘇格拉底，被雅典的公民大會判處死刑，罪名是：1. 對自然哲學進行研究而引進新神、不信舊神； 2. 具有「將弱的論證轉為強的論證」的詭辯能力並以此敗壞青年。就第一項指控的歷史背景來說，雖然並非所有自然哲學都抹去神明（或神性）的位置，但當時所盛行的原子論乃以原子機械式的必然運動取代神，並將神明及其相關的宗教概念歸因於人由於恐懼與敬畏的心理而虛構出來的，這對當時大部分的雅典人來說是很難接受的；至於第二項指控，這種「將弱的論證轉為強的論證」的詭辯能力在當時是智者所教授的演說術技巧，雖然它只問輸贏不問真理的特性對社會造成許多疑慮，但因為能讓人們在議會或法庭贏得論辯而受到歡迎，所以仍有許多人捧上大把鈔票去學習，尤其是許多想踏上仕途的年輕人。對於這兩項指控，蘇格拉底認為，皆是起因於人們對他的誤解。

　　這誤解從何而來？其實是來自蘇格拉底的哲學活動 (Socratic Inquiry)。對於智者在人的德性—善及其相關論點（例如德性可透過金錢買賣獲得）

上的看法，蘇格拉底是質疑的，為了釐清與正確指出人的真正德性—善，蘇格拉底開啟他直到生命盡頭仍在實踐的哲學活動：「只要我一息尚存，絕不會放棄追求智慧或停止規勸你們，並向所遇到的每個人指出真理。……我所做的無非是勸說你們，不論是年輕人或是老年人，毋須關心身體與財富更甚於自己靈魂的善，財富不會帶來德性，但德性會帶來財富以及其他種種對所有人而言是善的東西。」(Plato, *Apology of Socrates* 29d-30b) 於是，為了敦促人們關心自己靈魂的美善，蘇格拉底常常在市場、體育館等公開場合，以對話的方式，就善、正義、勇敢與虔誠等等道德與政治議題與人們進行討論，希望人們能由此去反思到自己在思考與行動時所依據的原理到底是什麼，亦即去檢驗自己的生命 (self-examination)，不要渾渾噩噩地任由矛盾粗陋的言行支配自己的人生，而是相反地，要成為對自己靈魂的美善有真確認識的人，也就是，能認識真正的自己。

在進行這樣的哲學活動時，蘇格拉底常以自己無知為由要求對話者能對所談論的主題（例如勇敢），給予「定義」(definition)，因為定義乃作為「典範」(pattern)，能給予我們一個「判準」(standard) 來判斷某人或某行為是否是勇敢的；然而，對定義的追尋在這哲學活動裡常以失敗告終，那原本自認擁有相關知識的對話者，其所提出的觀點在蘇格拉底與他一步步地交互詰問中 (cross-examination)，被揭露為自我矛盾而陷入困惑的處境，於是，雅典人懷疑蘇格拉底似乎具有像智者一樣的詭辯技巧，並將此技巧教給追隨他的年輕人並進而敗壞了他們；然而，雅典人並不明白，陷入困惑的處境只是此哲學活動的第一步，它能消除人們的自得意滿，而能產生真切的反省，進而認清自己懂什麼不懂什麼，如此才能啟動真正的反思，踏上追求真理的正確道路，在謙和、努力的認真思考當中獲得對美善靈魂的真確認識。

　　這樣的哲學活動其實也說明為什麼蘇格拉底總是推說他什麼都不懂、沒有什麼可教給人的：因為這種對美善靈魂的真確認識實際上是一種能洞察各種事物的善惡的價值判斷能力，是內在於自己靈魂裡的一種能洞悉善惡價值的理性能力，它並無法像其他學科那樣可以藉由複製與記憶而加以傳遞而有，這種複製地傳遞就好像我們不加思索地接受某個長久以來已由社會所認可的道德慣例並實踐之，但是，這對蘇格拉底來說並不是知識 (knowledge)，而只是意見 (belief)，這種意見即使為真，但若我們並沒有自覺地去鑒察此道德慣例背後的根本道理與價值，那麼便很容易受到外界的動搖而做出錯誤的判斷與決定，因此，蘇格拉底認為，唯有透過不斷交互詰問的哲學對話，才能持續鍛鍊靈魂裡的這種能鑒察善惡價值的理性能力於最佳狀態，這絕不是像智者那樣可用金錢交易而傳遞獲得的。值得一提的是，雅典人控告蘇格拉底引進的新神，其實正是這存在於靈魂裡能鑒察善惡的理性（參見 Plato, *Apology of Socrates* 31c-d），蘇格拉底沒有聲嘶力竭地斥責他的雅典同胞誤會他、冤枉他、讓他蒙受死亡威脅，而是溫和堅定的讓自己靈魂裡的這個神聖的聲音繼續引領他直到生命盡頭。

文本：

Apology of Socrates[1]

28a-34b

[28a] Well then, men of Athens, that I am not a wrongdoer according to Meletus's indictment, seems to me not to need much of a defense, but what has been said is enough. But you may be assured that what I said before is true, that great hatred has arisen against me and in the minds of many persons. And this it is which will cause my condemnation, if it is to cause it, not Meletus or Anytus, but the prejudice and dislike of the many. This has condemned many other good men, and I think will do so; [28b] and there is no danger that it will stop with me. But perhaps someone might say: "Are you then not ashamed, Socrates, of having followed such a pursuit, that you are now in danger of being put to death as a result?" But I should make to him a just reply: "You do not speak well, Sir, if you think a man in whom there is even a little merit ought to consider danger of life or death, and not rather regard this only, when he does things, whether the things he does are right or wrong and the acts of a good or a bad man. For according to your argument all the demigods [28c] would be bad who died at Troy, including the son of Thetis, who so despised danger, in comparison with enduring any disgrace, that when his mother (and she was a goddess) said to him, as he was eager to slay Hector, something like this, I believe, "My son, if you avenge the death of your friend Patroclus and kill Hector, you yourself shall die; for straightway, after Hector, is death appointed unto you;" he, when he heard this, made light of death and danger, [28d] and feared much more to live as a

---

[1] Trans. by Harold North Fowler, *Loeb Classical Library*, No. 36, vol. 1, Harvard University Press, 1914.

coward and not to avenge his friends, and said, "Straightway may I die, after doing vengeance upon the wrongdoer, that I may not stay here, jeered at beside the curved ships, a burden of the earth.". Do you think he considered death and danger? For thus it is, men of Athens, in truth; wherever a man stations himself, thinking it is best to be there, or is stationed by his commander, there he must, as it seems to me, remain and run his risks, considering neither death nor any other thing more than disgrace. So I should have done a terrible thing, [28e] if, when the commanders whom you chose to command me stationed me, both at Potidaea and at Amphipolis and at Delium, I remained where they stationed me, like anybody else, and ran the risk of death, but when the god gave me a station, as I believed and understood, with orders to spend my life in philosophy and in examining myself and others, [29a] then I were to desert my post through fear of death or anything else whatsoever. It would be a terrible thing, and truly one might then justly hale me into court, on the charge that I do not believe that there are gods, since I disobey the oracle and fear death and think I am wise when I am not. For to fear death, gentlemen, is nothing else than to think one is wise when one is not; for it is thinking one knows what one does not know. For no one knows whether death be not even the greatest of all blessings to man, but they fear it as if they knew that it is the greatest of evils. [29b] And is not this the most reprehensible form of ignorance, that of thinking one knows what one does not know? Perhaps, gentlemen, in this matter also I differ from other men in this way, and if I were to say that I am wiser in anything, it would be in this, that not knowing very much about the other world, I do not think I know. But I do know that it is evil and disgraceful to do wrong and to disobey him who is better than I, whether he be god or man. So I shall never fear or avoid those things concerning which I do not know whether they are good or bad rather than those which I know are bad. And therefore, even if [29c] you acquit me now and are not convinced by Anytus, who said that either I ought not to have been brought to trial at all, or since was brought to trial, I must certainly be put to death, adding that if I were acquitted your sons would all be utterly ruined by practicing what I teach—if you should say to me in reply to this: "Socrates, this time we will not do as Anytus says, but we will let you go, on this condition, however, that you no longer spend your time in this investigation or in philosophy, and if you are caught doing so again you shall die"; [29d] if you should let me go on this condition which I have mentioned, I should say to you, "Men of Athens, I respect and love you, but I shall obey the god rather than you, and while I live and am able to continue, I shall never give up philosophy or stop exhorting you and pointing out the truth to any one of you whom I may meet, saying in my accustomed way: "Most excellent man, are you who are a citizen of Athens, the greatest of cities and the most famous for wisdom and power, not ashamed to care for the acquisition of wealth [29e] and for reputation and honor, when you neither care nor take thought for wisdom and truth and the perfection of your soul?" And if any of you argues the point, and says he does care, I shall not let him go at once, nor shall I go away, but I shall question and examine and cross-examine him, and if I find that he does not possess virtue, but says he does, I shall rebuke him for scorning [30a] the things that are of most importance and caring more for what is of less worth. This I shall do to whomever I meet, young and old, foreigner and citizen, but most to the citizens, inasmuch as you are more nearly related to me. For know that the god commands me to do this, and I believe that no greater good ever came to pass in the city than my service to the god. For I go about doing nothing else than urging you, young and old, not to care for your persons or your property [30b] more than for the perfection of your souls, or even so much; and I tell you that virtue does not come from money, but from virtue comes money and all other good things to man, both to the individual and to the state. If by saying these things I corrupt the youth, these things must be injurious; but if anyone asserts that I say other things than these, he says what is untrue. Therefore I say to you, men of Athens, either do as Anytus tells you, or not, and either acquit me, or not, knowing that I shall not change my conduct even if I am [30c] to die many times over. Do not make a disturbance, men of Athens; continue to do what I asked of you, not to interrupt my speech by disturbances, but to hear me; and I believe you will profit by hearing. Now I am going to say some things to you at which you will perhaps cry out; but do not do so by any means. For know that if you kill me, I being such a man as I say I am, you will not injure me so much as yourselves; for neither Meletus nor Anytus could injure me; [30d] that would be impossible, for I believe it is not God's will that a better man be injured by a worse. He might, however, perhaps kill me or banish me or disfranchise me; and perhaps he thinks he would thus inflict great injuries upon me, and others may think so, but I do not; I think he does himself a much greater injury by doing what he is doing now—killing a man unjustly. And so, men of Athens, I am now making my defense not for my own sake, as one might imagine, but far more for yours, that you may not by condemning me err in your treatment of the gift the God gave you. [30e] For if you put me to death, you will not easily find another, who, to use a rather absurd figure, attaches himself to the city as a gadfly to a horse, which, though large and well bred, is sluggish on account of his size and needs to be aroused by stinging. I think the god fastened me upon the city in some such capacity, and I go about arousing, [31a] and urging and reproaching each one of you, constantly alighting upon you everywhere the whole day long. Such another is not likely to come to you, gentlemen; but if you take my advice, you will spare me. But you, perhaps, might be angry, like people awakened from a nap, and might slap me, as Anytus advises, and easily kill me; then you would pass the rest of your lives in slumber, unless God, in his care for you, should send someone else to sting you. And that I am, as I say, a kind of gift from the god,

[31b] you might understand from this; for I have neglected all my own affairs and have been enduring the neglect of my concerns all these years, but I am always busy in your interest, coming to each one of you individually like a father or an elder brother and urging you to care for virtue; now that is not like human conduct. If I derived any profit from this and received pay for these exhortations, there would be some sense in it; but now you yourselves see that my accusers, though they accuse me of everything else in such a shameless way, have not been able to work themselves up to such a pitch of shamelessness [31c] as to produce a witness to testify that I ever exacted or asked pay of anyone. For I think I have a sufficient witness that I speak the truth, namely, my poverty. Perhaps it may seem strange that I go about and interfere in other people's affairs to give this advice in private, but do not venture to come before your assembly and advise the state. But the reason for this, as you have heard me say [31d] at many times and places, is that something divine and spiritual comes to me, the very thing which Meletus ridiculed in his indictment. I have had this from my childhood; it is a sort of voice that comes to me, and when it comes it always holds me back from what I am thinking of doing, but never urges me forward. This it is which opposes my engaging in politics. And I think this opposition is a very good thing; for you may be quite sure, men of Athens, that if I had undertaken to go into politics, I should have been put to death long ago and should have done [31e] no good to you or to myself. And do not be angry with me for speaking the truth; the fact is that no man will save his life who nobly opposes you or any other populace and prevents many unjust and illegal things from happening in the state. [32a] A man who really fights for the right, if he is to preserve his life for even a little while, must be a private citizen, not a public man. I will give you powerful proofs of this, not mere words, but what you honor more,—actions. And listen to what happened to me, that you may be convinced that I would never yield to any one, if that was wrong, through fear of death, but

would die rather than yield. The tale I am going to tell you is ordinary and commonplace, but true. [32b] I, men of Athens, never held any other office in the state, but I was a senator; and it happened that my tribe held the presidency when you wished to judge collectively, not severally, the ten generals who had failed to gather up the slain after the naval battle; this was illegal, as you all agreed afterwards. At that time I was the only one of the prytanes who opposed doing anything contrary to the laws, and although the orators were ready to impeach and arrest me, and though you urged them with shouts to do so, I thought [32c] I must run the risk to the end with law and justice on my side, rather than join with you when your wishes were unjust, through fear of imprisonment or death. That was when the democracy still existed; and after the oligarchy was established, the Thirty sent for me with four others to come to the rotunda and ordered us to bring Leon the Salaminian from Salamis to be put to death. They gave many such orders to others also, because they wished to implicate as many in their crimes as they could. Then I, however, [32d] showed again, by action, not in word only, that I did not care a whit for death if that be not too rude an expression, but that I did care with all my might not to do anything unjust or unholy. For that government, with all its power, did not frighten me into doing anything unjust, but when we came out of the rotunda, the other four went to Salamis and arrested Leon, but I simply went home; and perhaps I should have been put to death for it, if the government had not [32e] quickly been put down. Of these facts you can have many witnesses. Do you believe that I could have lived so many years if I had been in public life and had acted as a good man should act, lending my aid to what is just and considering that of the highest importance? Far from it, men of Athens; nor could [33a] any other man. But you will find that through all my life, both in public, if I engaged in any public activity, and in private, I have always been the same as now, and have never yielded to any one wrongly, whether it were any other person or any of those who are said by my traducers to be my pupils. But I was never any one's teacher. If any one, whether young or old, wishes to hear me speaking and pursuing my mission, I have never objected, [33b] nor do I converse only when I am paid and not otherwise, but I offer myself alike to rich and poor; I ask questions, and whoever wishes may answer and hear what I say. And whether any of them turns out well or ill, I should not justly be held responsible, since I never promised or gave any instruction to any of them; but if any man says that he ever learned or heard anything privately from me, which all the others did not, be assured that he is lying. But why then do some people love [33c] to spend much of their time with me? You have heard the reason, men of Athens; for I told you the whole truth; it is because they like to listen when those are examined who think they are wise and are not so; for it is amusing. But, as I believe, I have been commanded to do this by the God through oracles and dreams and in every way in which any man was ever commanded by divine power to do anything whatsoever. This, Athenians, is true and easily tested. For if I am corrupting some of the young men [33d] and have corrupted others, surely some of them who have grown older, if they recognize that I ever gave them any bad advice when they were young, ought now to have come forward to accuse me. Or if they did not wish to do it themselves, some of their relatives—fathers or brothers or other kinsfolk—ought now to tell the facts. And there are many of them present, whom I see; first Crito here, [33e] who is of my own age and my own deme and father of Critobulus, who is also present; then there is Lysanias the Sphettian, father of Aeschines, who is here; and also Antiphon of Cephisus, father of Epigenes. Then here are others whose brothers joined in my conversations, Nicostratus, son of Theozotides and brother of Theodotus (now Theodotus is dead, so he could not stop him by entreaties), and Paralus, son of Demodocus; Theages was his brother; and [34a] Adimantus, son of Aristo, whose brother is Plato here; and Aeantodorus, whose brother Apollodorus is present. And I can mention to you many others, some one of whom Meletus ought certainly to have produced as a witness in his speech; but if he forgot it then, let him do so now; I yield the floor to him, and let him say, if he has any such testimony. But you will find that the exact opposite is the case, gentlemen, and that they are all ready to aid me, the man who corrupts and injures their relatives, as Meletus and Anytus say. [34b] Now those who are themselves corrupted might have some motive in aiding me; but what reason could their relatives have, who are not corrupted and are already older men, unless it be the right and true reason, that they know that Meletus is lying and I am speaking the truth?

問題討論：

1. 蘇格拉底如何論說他的生命之道是什麼？為什麼他自認為自己的生命之道是神明賜給城邦的禮物？

2. 為什麼蘇格拉底認為，真正為正義奮鬥的人，如果要公開從政，必定活不久？ 你認為蘇格拉底四處奔跑、私下裡向人提供意見或與人討論關於正義…等諸 價值的事情，是否是政治活動？如果 "是" ［或 "不是"］，那麼，你認為理由是什麼？

3. 什麼是蘇格拉底的「認識你自己」？你覺得有道理嗎？

延伸閱讀：

1. Brickhouse, Thomas C. and Nicholas D. Smith, *The Trial and Execution of Socrates*, Oxford, 2002.

2. Dodds, E. R., *The Greeks and the Irrational*, Berkeley, 1951.

3. Guthrie, W. K. C., *The Greeks and Their Gods*, Boston, 1950.

五、蘇格拉底與柏拉圖（二）

蘇富芝

單元旨要：

　　蘇格拉底的哲學活動有些困境：我們有可能會去尋找「所不知道的」嗎？如果不知道要找的東西，那麼，就根本不會去找，因此不可能會有這樣的哲學活動；再來，就算哲學活動進行了，在這當中，蘇格拉底想藉由他的對話者所初步提供的定義，例如關於「勇敢」，來判斷某些行為是否是勇敢的，然而，這裡有個弔詭是，他們此時此刻並不知道什麼是勇敢（亦即「勇敢」的真正定義），那麼，他們要如何指出哪些行為是勇敢呢？另外，在尋找定義時，蘇格拉底要求他的對話者不要以感覺所觀察到的個例來提供定義，因為這些個例並無法完整說明所要定義的，例如，若以「無畏」(fearless) 來定義「勇敢」，也許有些情況適用，但是，一個對眼前危險毫無所悉而無畏的愚人也能是勇敢的嗎？所以，蘇格拉底認為，定義無法從許多個例的列舉中獲得，而是需要一個能放諸四海皆準的典範，那麼，如果這個典範不能來自感覺所觀察到的，那這些典範的存有位階應來自哪裡？雖然蘇格拉底畢生實踐這個哲學活動，但他從未說明這個方法是如何運作而為有效，而這正是柏拉圖哲學的起點。

　　針對此，柏拉圖提出「學習即回憶」的論點，亦即所有的學習皆只是回憶：儘管人的靈魂在所謂的生死輪迴中流轉，但，實際為不死的，靈魂在出生前便已學習且認識了真理，出生後只要藉由那以正確方式進行的

對話問答（亦即蘇格拉底交互詰問的哲學活動），便能喚起我們早已認識的真理。柏拉圖在《曼諾篇》(Meno) 為此舉例：作為對話主角的蘇格拉底與一位未受教育的童僕進行對話，蘇格拉底借助沙地上的圖表，在有技巧的問答中來引導童僕去理解 —— 若要獲得原正方形兩倍大面積的正方形，那此兩倍大正方形的邊長應為何？在這當中，沒有知識的童僕從自身所持的從感覺而來的真假意見開始，透過蘇格拉底正確有技巧的問答，童僕在衝突矛盾的意見中能逐步剔除假意見而保留真意見，雖然中間曾陷入困惑，但到最後仍能說出正確的意見，而如果能繼續不斷地以不同方式探問童僕，直到童僕回憶起「關於原因的合理考慮」(the calculation of reason, reasoned explanation)，並以此將這些真意見束縛住，那麼這受束縛的真意見便轉為持守在靈魂裡的知識。而這能將真意見束縛為不動搖的知識的「原因」，柏拉圖稱之為「相」(Form, eidos)，這也正是蘇格拉底對於定義所要求的典範：凡是由感覺而來的皆無法免於變動，也就是，由感覺而來的某個美的也可以是醜，大的也可以是小，虔誠的也可以為不虔誠……等等，但是，「相」卻能免除這些矛盾而永恆為一，因為「相」是獨立於感覺之外，我們無法透過肉體的感官知覺去知道「相」，只有透過靈魂裡的理性才能掌握。

柏拉圖認為，這個追求真理與知識的活動（「學習即回憶」）正能說明蘇格拉底的哲學活動是可能的，並指出，這樣的學習並不是如同那些智者所說的，要將知識放進空白的靈魂裡，如同將視力放進盲眼裡一樣，而是，要將整個靈魂轉向，使原本便具有視力的靈魂之眼（亦即理性）能轉向正確的方向 (Plato, Republic 518c-d)，也就是，不再看生滅變動的感覺者，而是專注於永恆同一的「相」，並在靈魂之眼的努力回憶中（亦即蘇格拉底交互詰問的哲學活動），以「善之相」為最終目的，因為唯有能真確認識善，才能對各種事物的價值有正確的判斷。

　　「學習即回憶」的論點不僅肯定蘇格拉底哲學活動的可能性，也讓我們轉而去關注到底對我們自己來說什麼是最重要的：如果靈魂是不死的且是真正的自己，那麼，能對靈魂有所裨益的，就絕不是那從屬於身體的慾望、財富、政治權力……等等，而是靈魂是否是善良或是邪惡，正義或是不正義。蘇格拉底認為，若要真正傷害一個人，那麼，所要做的並不是讓他在身體或金錢上受到傷害或損失，而是要讓他成為一個做盡壞事的邪惡的靈魂 (Plato, *Apology of Socrates* 30c-d)，這樣的靈魂雖然表面上因為做不正義的事而吃香喝辣，看起來似乎過得很好，但實際上是一個因放縱自己慾望而總是處在不滿、痛苦與害怕當中的不幸福者。

　　雖然我們並未在此傳達柏拉圖哲學的所有面向，但是，若能認知到柏拉圖整個哲學的起點與核心皆來自於他的老師蘇格拉底，那麼，我們才能真正了解柏拉圖。當柏拉圖在《國家篇》(*Republic*) 處理這兩個主題時 [1. 完全正義的人與完全不正義的人（亦即受盡苦楚的正義之人與享盡榮華富貴的不正義之人），究竟誰是幸福的？以及 2. 哲人王的養成教育]，他心中總是以蘇格拉底來作為他整個哲學論證之為可能的客觀依據。

文本：

Meno[1]

70a-79e

[70a]

Meno

Can you tell me, Socrates, whether virtue can be taught, or is acquired by practice, not teaching? Or if neither by practice nor by learning, whether it comes to mankind by nature or in some other way?

Socrates

Meno, of old the Thessalians were famous and admired among the Greeks for their riding and [70b] their riches; but now they have a name, I believe, for wisdom also, especially your friend Aristippus's people, the Larisaeans. For this you have to thank Gorgias: for when he came to that city he made the leading men of the Aleuadae—among them your lover Aristippus—and the Thessalians generally enamored of wisdom. Nay more, he has given you the regular habit of answering any chance question in a fearless, magnificent manner, as befits those who know: [70c] for he sets the example of offering himself to be questioned by any Greek who chooses, and on any point one likes, and he has an answer for everybody. Now in this place, my dear Meno, we have a contrary state of things: [71a] a drought of wisdom, as it were,

---

[1] Trans. by W. R. M. Lamb, *Loeb Classical Library*, No. 165, vol. 2, Harvard University Press, 1924.

has come on; and it seems as though wisdom had deserted our borders in favour of yours. You have only to ask one of our people a question such as that, and he will be sure to laugh and say: Stranger, you must think me a specially favoured mortal, to be able to tell whether virtue can be taught, or in what way it comes to one: so far am I from knowing whether it can be taught or not, that I actually do not even know what the thing itself, virtue, is at all. [71b] And I myself, Meno, am in the same case; I share my townsmen's poverty in this matter: I have to reproach myself with an utter ignorance about virtue; and if I do not know what a thing is, how can I know what its nature may be? Or do you imagine it possible, if one has no cognizance at all of Meno, that one could know whether he is handsome or rich or noble, or the reverse of these? Do you suppose that one could?

Meno

Not I. But is it true, Socrates, [71c] that you do not even know what virtue is? Are we to return home with this report of you?

Socrates

Not only this, my friend, but also that I never yet came across anybody who did know, in my opinion.

Meno

What? You did not meet Gorgias when he was here?

Socrates

I did.

Meno

And you didn't consider that he knew?

Socrates

I have not a very good memory, Meno, so I cannot tell at the moment how he struck me then. It may be that he did know, and that you know what he said: [71d] remind me therefore how he expressed it; or if you like, make your own statement, for I expect you share his views.

Meno

I do.

Socrates

Then let us pass him over, since in fact he is not present, and do you tell me, in heaven's name, what is your own account of virtue. Speak out frankly, that I may find myself the victim of a most fortunate falsehood, if you and Gorgias prove to have knowledge of it, while I have said that I never yet came across anyone who had. [71e]

Meno

Why, there is no difficulty, Socrates, in telling. First of all, if you take the virtue of a man, it is easily stated that a man's virtue is this—that he be competent to manage the affairs of his city, and to manage them so as to benefit his friends and harm his enemies, and to take care to avoid suffering harm himself. Or take a woman's virtue: there is no difficulty in describing it as the duty of ordering the house well, looking after the property indoors, and obeying her husband. And the child has another virtue—one for the female, and one for the male; and there is another for elderly men—one, if you like, for freemen, [72a] and yet another for slaves. And there are very many other virtues besides, so that one cannot be at a loss to explain what virtue is; for it is according to each activity and age that every one of us, in whatever we do, has his virtue; and the same, I take it, Socrates, will hold also of vice.

Socrates

I seem to be in a most lucky way, Meno; for in seeking one virtue I have discovered a whole swarm of virtues there in your keeping. Now, Meno, to follow this figure of a swarm, [72b] suppose I should ask you what is the real nature of the bee, and you replied that there are many different kinds of bees, and I rejoined: Do you say it is by being bees that they are of many and various kinds and differ from each other, or does their difference lie not in that, but in something else—for example, in their beauty or size or some other quality? Tell me, what would be your answer to this question?

Meno

Why, this—that they do not differ, as bees, the one from the other. [72c]

Socrates

And if I went on to say: Well now, there is this that I want you to tell me, Meno: what do you call the quality by which they do not differ, but are all alike? You could find me an answer, I presume?

Meno

I could.

Socrates

And likewise also with the virtues, however many and various they may be, they all have one common character whereby they are virtues, and on which one would of course be wise to keep an eye when one is giving a definitive answer to the question of what virtue really is. [72d] You take my meaning, do you not?

Meno

My impression is that I do; but still I do not yet grasp the meaning of the question as I could wish.

Socrates

Is it only in the case of virtue, do you think, Meno, that one can say there is one kind belonging to a man, another to a woman, and so on with the rest, or is it just the same, too, in the case of health and size and strength? Do you consider that there is one health for a man, and another for a woman? Or, wherever we find health, is it of the same character universally, [72e] in a man or in anyone else?

Meno

I think that health is the same, both in man and in woman.

Socrates

Then is it not so with size and strength also? If a woman is strong, she will be strong by reason of the same form and the same strength; by "the same" I mean that strength does not differ as strength, whether it be in a man or in a woman. Or do you think there is any difference?

Meno

I do not.

[73a]

Socrates

And will virtue, as virtue, differ at all whether it be in a child or in an elderly person, in a woman or in a man?

Meno

I feel somehow, Socrates, that here we cease to be on the same ground as in those other cases.

Socrates

Why? Were you not saying that a man's virtue is to manage a state well, and a woman's a house?

Meno

I was.

Socrates

And is it possible to manage a state well, or a house, or anything at all, if you do not manage it temperately and justly? [73b]

Meno

Surely not.

Socrates

Then whoever manages temperately and justly will manage with temperance and justice?

Meno

That must be.

Socrates

Then both the woman and the man require the same qualities of justice and temperance, if they are to be good.

Meno

Evidently.

Socrates

And what of a child or an old man? Can they ever hope to be good if they are intemperate and unjust?

Meno

Surely not.

Socrates

Only if they are temperate and just?

Meno

Yes. [73c]

Socrates

So all mankind are good in the same way; for they become good when they acquire the same qualities.

Meno

So it seems.

Socrates

And I presume, if they had not the same virtue, they would not be good in the same way.

Meno

No, indeed.

Socrates

Seeing then that it is the same virtue in all cases, try and tell me, if you can recollect, what Gorgias—and you in agreement with him—say it is.

Meno

Simply that it is the power of governing mankind— [73d] if you want some single description to cover all cases.

Socrates

That is just what I am after. But is virtue the same in a child, Meno, and in a slave—an ability to govern each his master? And do you think he who governed would still be a slave?

Meno

I should say certainly not, Socrates.

Socrates

No, indeed, it would be unlikely, my excellent friend. And again, consider this further point: you say it is "to be able to govern"; shall we not add to that—"justly, not unjustly"?

Meno

Yes, I think so; for justice, Socrates, is virtue. [73e]

Socrates

Virtue, Meno, or a virtue?

Meno

What do you mean by that?

Socrates

What I would in any other case. To take roundness, for instance; I should call it a figure, and not figure pure and simple. And I should name it so because there are other figures as well.

Meno

You would be quite right—just as I say there are other virtues besides justice. [74a]

Socrates

What are they? Tell me. In the same way as I can tell you of other figures, if you request me, so do you tell me of other virtues.

Meno

Well then, courage, I consider, is a virtue, and temperance, and wisdom, and loftiness of mind; and there are a great many others.

Socrates

Once more, Meno, we are in the same plight: again we have found a number of virtues when we were looking for one, though not in the same way as we did just now; but the one that runs through them all, this we are not able to find. [74b]

Meno

No, for I am not yet able, Socrates, to follow your line of search, and find a single virtue common to all, as one can in other cases.

Socrates

And no wonder; but I will make an effort, so far as I can, to help us onward. You understand, of course, that this principle of mine applies to everything: if someone asked you the question I put to you just now: What is figure, Meno? and you replied: Roundness; and then he said, as I did: Is roundness figure or a figure? I suppose you would answer: A figure.

Meno

Certainly. [74c]

Socrates

And for this reason—that there are other figures as well?

Meno

Yes.

Socrates

And if he went on to ask you of what sort they were, you would tell him?

Meno

I would.

Socrates

And if he asked likewise what color is, and on your answering "white" your questioner then rejoined: Is "white" color or a color? your reply would be: A color; because there are other colors besides.

Meno

It would.

Socrates

And if he bade you mention other colors, [74d] you would tell him of others that are colors just as much as white?

Meno

Yes.

Socrates

Now suppose that, like me, he pursued the argument and said: We are always arriving at a variety of things, but let me have no more of that: since you call these many things by one single name, and say they are figures, every one of them, even when they are opposed to one another, tell me what is that which comprises round and straight alike, and which you call figure— [74e] including straight equally with round under that term. For that is your statement, is it not?

Meno

It is.

Socrates

And in making it, do you mean to say that round is no more round than straight, or straight no more straight than round?

Meno

No, to be sure, Socrates.

Socrates

What you mean is that the round shape is no more a figure than the straight, or the straight than the round.

Meno

Quite right.

Socrates

Then what can this thing be, which bears the name of figure? Try and tell me. Suppose that, on being asked this question by someone, [75a] either about figure or about color, you had replied: Why, I don't so much as understand what you want, sir, or even know what you are saying: he might well have shown surprise, and said: Do you not understand that I am looking for that which is the same common element in all these things? Or would you still be unable to reply, Meno, if you were approached on other terms, and were asked: What is it that is common to the round and the straight and everything else that you call figures—the same in all? Try and tell me it will be good practice for your answer about virtue. [75b]

Meno

No, it is you who must answer, Socrates.

Socrates

You wish me to do you the favour?

Meno

By all means.

Socrates

And then you will agree to take your turn and answer me on virtue?

Meno

I will.

Socrates

Well then, I must make the effort, for it is worth our while.

Meno

Certainly.

Socrates

Come now, let me try and tell you what figure is. Just consider if you accept this description of it: figure, let us say, is the only existing thing that is found always following color. Are you satisfied, or are you looking for something different? I am sure I should be content with a similar account of virtue from you. [75c]

Meno

But it is such a silly one, Socrates.

Socrates

How do you mean?

Meno

Well, figure, as I understand by your account, is what always follows color. Very good; but if someone said he did not know color, and was in the same difficulty about it as about figure, what answer do you suppose would have come from you?

Socrates

The truth, from me; and if my questioner were a professor of the eristic and contentious sort, I should say to him: [75d] I have made my statement; if it is wrong, your business is to examine and refute it. But if, like you and me on this occasion, we were friends and chose to have a discussion together, I should have to reply in some milder tone more suited to dialectic. The more dialectical way, I suppose, is not merely to answer what is true, but also to make use of those points which the questioned person acknowledges he knows. And this is the way in which I shall now try to argue with you. Tell me, is there something you call an end? Such a thing, I mean, [75e] as a limit, or extremity—I use all these terms in the same sense, though I daresay Prodicus might quarrel with us. But you, I am sure, refer to a thing as terminated or ended: something of that sort is what I mean—nothing complicated.

Meno

Yes, I do, and I think I grasp your meaning. [76a]

Socrates

Well then, you speak of a surface, and also of a solid—the terms employed in geometrical problems?

Meno

I do.

Socrates

So now you are able to comprehend from all this what I mean by figure. In every instance of figure I call that figure in which the solid ends; and I may put that more succinctly by saying that figure is "limit of solid."

Meno

And what do you say of color, Socrates?

Socrates

How overbearing of you, Meno, to press an old man with demands for answers, when you will not trouble yourself [76b] to recollect and tell me what account Gorgias gives of virtue!

Meno

When you have answered my question, Socrates, I will answer yours.

Socrates

One might tell even blindfolded, Meno, by the way you discuss, that you are handsome and still have lovers.

Meno

Why so?

Socrates

Because you invariably speak in a peremptory tone, after the fashion of spoilt beauties, holding as they do a despotic power so long as their bloom is on them. You have also, I daresay, [76c] made a note of my weakness for handsome people. So I will indulge you, and answer.

Meno

You must certainly indulge me.

Socrates

Then would you like me to answer you in the manner of Gorgias, which you would find easiest to follow?

Meno

I should like that, of course.

Socrates

Do not both of you say there are certain effluences of existent things, as Empedocles held?

Meno

Certainly.

Socrates

And passages into which and through which the effluences pass?

Meno

To be sure.

Socrates

And some of the effluences fit into various passages, [76d] while some are too small or too large?

Meno

That is so.

Socrates

And further, there is what you call sight?

Meno

Yes.

Socrates

So now "conceive my meaning," as Pindar says: color is an effluence of figures, commensurate with sight and sensible.

Meno

Your answer, Socrates, seems to me excellently put.

Socrates

Yes, for I expect you find its terms familiar; and at the same time I fancy you observe that it enables you to tell what sound and smell are, and numerous other [76e] things of the kind.

Meno

Certainly.

Socrates

It is an answer in the high poetic style, Meno, and so more agreeable to you than that about figure.

Meno

Yes, it is.

Socrates

But yet, son of Alexidemus, I am inclined to think the other was the better of the two; and I believe you also would prefer it, if you were not compelled, as you were saying yesterday, to go away before the mysteries, and could stay awhile and be initiated. [77a]

Meno

But I should stay, Socrates, if you would give me many such answers.

Socrates

Well then, I will spare no endeavor, both for your sake and for my own, to continue in that style; but I fear I may not succeed in keeping for long on that level. But come now, you in your turn must try and fulfil your promise by telling me what virtue is in a general way; and you must stop producing a plural from the singular, as the wags say whenever one breaks something, but leave virtue [77b] whole and sound, and tell me what it is. The pattern you have now got from me.

Meno

Well, in my view, Socrates, virtue is, in the poet's words, "to rejoice in things honorable and be able for them"; and that, I say, is virtue—to desire what is honorable and be able to procure it.

Socrates

Do you say that he who desires the honorable is desirous of the good?

Meno

Certainly.

Socrates

Implying that there are some who desire the evil, and others the good? Do not all men, [77c] in your opinion, my dear sir, desire the good?

Meno

I think not.

Socrates

There are some who desire the evil?

Meno

Yes.

Socrates

Thinking the evil to be good, do you mean, or actually recognizing it to be evil, and desiring it nevertheless?

Meno

Both, I believe.

Socrates

Do you really believe, Meno, that a man knows the evil to be evil, and still desires it?

Meno

Certainly.

Socrates

What do you mean by "desires"? Desires the possession of it? [77d]

Meno

Yes; what else could it be?

Socrates

And does he think the evil benefits him who gets it, or does he know that it harms him who has it?

Meno

There are some who think the evil is a benefit, and others who know that it does harm.

Socrates

And, in your opinion, do those who think the evil a benefit know that it is evil?

Meno

I do not think that at all.

Socrates

Obviously those who are ignorant of the evil do not desire it, but only what they supposed [77e] to be good, though it is really evil; so that those who are ignorant of it and think it good are really desiring the good. Is not that so?

Meno

It would seem to be so in their case.

Socrates

Well now, I presume those who, as you say, desire the evil, and consider that the evil harms him who gets it, know that they will be harmed by it?

Meno

They needs must. [78a]

Socrates

But do they not hold that those who are harmed are miserable in proportion to the harm they suffer?

Meno

That too must be.

Socrates

And are not the miserable ill-starred?

Meno

I think so.

Socrates

Then is there anyone who wishes to be miserable and ill-starred?

Meno

I do not suppose there is, Socrates.

Socrates

No one, then, Meno, desires evil, if no one desires to be such an one: for what is being miserable but desiring evil and obtaining it? [78b]

Meno

It seems that what you say is true, Socrates, and that nobody desires evil.

Socrates

Well now, you were saying a moment ago that virtue is the desire and ability for good?

Meno

Yes, I was.

Socrates

One part of the statement—the desire—belongs to our common nature, and in this respect one man is no better than another?

Meno

Apparently.

Socrates

But it is plain that if one man is not better than another in this, he must be superior in the ability.

Meno

Certainly.

Socrates

Then virtue, it seems by your account, [78c] is ability to procure goods.

Meno

I entirely agree, Socrates, with the view which you now take of the matter.

Socrates

Then let us see whether your statement is true in another respect; for very likely you may be right. You say virtue is the ability to procure goods?

Meno

I do.

Socrates

And do you not mean by goods such things as health and wealth?

Meno

Yes, and I include the acquisition of gold and silver, and of state honors and offices.

Socrates

Are there any things besides this sort, that you class as goods?

Meno

No, I refer only to everything of that sort. [78d]

Socrates

Very well: procuring gold and silver is virtue, according to Meno, the ancestral friend of the Great King. Tell me, do you add to such procuring, Meno, that it is to be done justly and piously, or is this indifferent to you, but even though a man procures these things unjustly, do you call them virtue all the same?

Meno

Surely not, Socrates.

Socrates

Rather, vice.

Meno

Yes, of course.

Socrates

Then it seems that justice or temperance or holiness or some other part of virtue must accompany the procuring of these things; [78e] otherwise it will not be virtue, though it provides one with goods.

Meno

Yes, for how, without these, could it be virtue?

Socrates

And not to procure gold and silver, when it would be unjust—what we call the want of such things—is virtue, is it not?

Meno

Apparently.

Socrates

So the procuring of this sort of goods will be no more virtue than the want of them; but it seems that whatever comes accompanied by justice will be virtue, [79a] and whatever comes without any such quality, vice.

Meno

I agree that it must be as you say.

Socrates

And were we saying a little while ago that each of these things was a part of virtue—justice and temperance and the rest of them?

Meno

Yes.

Socrates

And here you are, Meno, making fun of me?

Meno

How so, Socrates?

Socrates

Because after my begging you not to break up virtue into small change, and giving you a pattern on which you should answer, you have ignored all this, and now tell me that virtue is [79b] the ability to procure good things with justice; and this, you tell me, is a part of virtue?

Meno

I do.

Socrates

Then it follows from your own admission that doing whatever one does with a part of virtue is itself virtue; for you say that justice is a part of virtue, and so is each of such qualities. You ask the meaning of my remark. It is that after my requesting you to speak of virtue as a whole, you say not a word as to what it is in itself, but tell me that every action is virtue provided that it is done [79c] with a part of virtue; as though you had told me what virtue is in the whole, and I must understand it forthwith—when you are really splitting it up into fragments! I think therefore that you must face the same question all over again, my dear Meno—What is virtue?—if we are to be told that every action accompanied by a part of virtue is virtue; for that is the meaning of the statement that every action accompanied by justice is virtue. Or do you not agree that you have to meet the same question afresh? Do you suppose that anyone can know a part of virtue when he does not know virtue itself?

Meno

No, I do not. [79d]

Socrates

And I daresay you remember, when I answered you a while ago about figure, how we rejected the sort of answer that attempts to proceed in terms which are still under inquiry and has not yet been admitted.

Meno

Yes, and we were right in rejecting it, Socrates.

Socrates

Well then, my good sir, you must not in your turn suppose that while the nature of virtue as a whole is still under inquiry you will explain it to anyone by replying in terms of its parts, or by any other statement [79e] on the same lines: you will only have to face the same question over again—What is this virtue, of which you are speaking all the time? Or do you see no force in what I say?

Meno

I think what you say is right.

Socrates

Then answer me again from the beginning: what do both you and your associate say that virtue is?

問題討論：

1. 蘇格拉底的哲學活動如何獲得柏拉圖所提出的「學習即回憶」的支持？

2. 請依據柏拉圖的《費多篇》(Phaedo) 來說明靈魂與相之間的關係。

3. 柏拉圖與蘇格拉底為什麼認為靈魂是真正的自己？請參考柏拉圖的《費多篇》或是《蘇格拉底自辯篇》或是其他對話錄。

延伸閱讀：

1. Allan Bloom, *The Republic of Plato*, 2nd edition, New York: Basic Books, 1991.

2. Seth Benardete (with translation), Allan Bloom and Seth Benardete (with commentaries), *Plato's Symposium*, Chicago, 2001.

3. Eric Voegelin, *Plato*, paperback edition, Missouri, 2000.

六、奧古斯丁——論時間與永恆

王志銘

單元旨要：

　　奧古斯丁生於西元 354 年北非（今阿爾及利亞）一個小地主家庭，母親莫妮卡為虔誠的基督徒，但從小叛逆的奧古斯丁卻排斥基督教信仰，十八歲時甚至生了一個私生子，隔年開始信奉摩尼教，與他的母親起衝突。之後便偷偷與友人不告而別離開家鄉前往羅馬。西元 380 年基督教解禁成為羅馬帝國境內可以公開宣傳的宗教，西元 392 年羅馬曾進一步禁止其他宗教，規定只能信仰基督教。奧古斯丁在西元 383 年抵達羅馬，當時摩尼教仍被禁止，而基督教卻已成了晉升上流社會非常重要的媒介。西元 385 年在他母親的逼迫下，奧古斯丁將同居十多年的女子遣送回北非托教會代為照顧，自己轉而跟一位才年僅十四歲的基督教貴族女子訂婚，婚前的兩年自己卻又與另一女子同居，沉浸肉慾歡樂之中。西元 386 年透過摩尼教教友引介，來到米蘭任職，在當地認識了當時基督教界最富盛名的學問僧米蘭主教 Ambrosius，在其引導下開始讀 Plotinus 與保羅書信集。西元 386 年秋季，由於長年鬱鬱寡歡，加上對摩尼教教主的徹底失望，身心陷入空前的危機，在一次身心俱疲非常痛苦的情境之中，偶然聽到嬰孩的聲音：「拿起來讀！」而衝回客房，翻開聖經讀到羅馬書 (13-13~14)：「不可荒宴醉酒，不可好色邪蕩，不可埋怨忌妒。而應回歸主耶穌，謹慎防身，勿使充滿肉慾。」從此便幡然悔改，決定過隱修的生活，不再與女人同房並放棄婚姻與職業，西元 387 年 4 月正式受洗成為基督

徒。之後與一群同好在北非共組隱修團，西元 391 年被按立為北非第二大港西坡城的主教，直到西元 430 年病死於汪達耳人入侵北非之際。

　　奧古斯丁著作甚豐，不僅著書駁斥摩尼教教義，並調停北非教派間的爭戰，自己也投身對抗基督教伯拉糾主義，長達二十多年的論戰，提出了「自由與恩典」、「嬰兒天生有罪」與「雙重預定論」等思想，對後世基督教神學產生極為深遠的影響。

　　下面這篇文章，選自奧古斯丁《懺悔錄》卷十一，主要是從基督教觀點出發探討「時間」的議題。「時間究竟是什麼？」這是古往今來一直困擾人類未曾止息的一個大哉問。大哲學家無不企圖嘗試去回答此一問題，而西方哲學史上對此問題做出重大貢獻的主要就是亞里斯多德、奧古斯丁與康德三人。亞里斯多德偏向從外在客觀物理世界的變化來觀察時間，康德則偏向從主觀純粹內感覺直觀的形式條件來說明時間，而奧古斯丁則是由外而內這一轉向的主要橋梁。奧古斯丁與亞里斯多德一樣，認為時間不等於物體之變化，但時間亦不可能離開變化去做出說明。但是奧古斯丁不像亞里斯多德停留在外在物體「運動所有的某種東西」或「就先後而言的運動的數目」來討論時間，而將這一先後秩序拉回到主觀心靈的「記憶」、「感覺」與「期望」來說明時間之度量，並且認為「現在是沒有絲毫長度的」。

　　奧古斯丁如果有幸生在當代，或許會修正「現在是沒有絲毫長度的」這一說法，因為現代物理學中的時間最小單位其實是一普朗克時間（大約是 5×10^{-44} 秒），也就是「現在其實是有絲毫長度的」，但這並不妨礙他繼續堅持時間只是「受造的」，並且與存在的受造物有著不可分割的關係。設使奧古斯丁贊同愛因斯坦的時間相對論，承認客觀物理向度中的時

間與物體的運動速度有著相對應的密切關係，他堅持的「沒有活動變化便沒有時間」這樣的命題依舊是可以成立的。奧古斯丁認為只當上帝創造無時間性的純全精神與渾沌無形的原質之後，才創造出會變形的因而遭受時間限制的人與物出來，並斬釘截鐵地說：「沒有活動變化，便沒有時間；而沒有形象便沒有變化。」

如果不特別在意奧古斯丁的基督教立場，仔細閱讀他對「時間」問題的諸多推斷，不難看出他心思之敏銳迥異常人。也難怪從中古到現代，無數的大哲學家喜歡在奧古斯丁的著作裡尋寶，連專門反駁奧古斯丁的當代英美分析哲學大師維根斯坦，口袋裡都時時揣著一本拉丁原文的「懺悔錄」。

最後值得注意的是，《懺悔錄》這本書的體裁，雖是獨白式的對著上帝傾訴與懺悔，卻詳述著奧古斯丁生平的珍貴回憶，與他思想的複雜轉折，讀來既引人入勝，卻又發人深省。

選讀文本：

【四】……天地高呼它們是受造的，因為它們在變化。凡不是受造而自己就存在的，在它身上就不可能出現之前無有而之後卻存有的東西，也就是不能有所謂變化的東西。

天地高喊著它們不是自造的：「我們所以有，是受造而有；在未有之前，我們並不存在，也不能自己創造自己。」

因此，主，是祢創造了天地；祢是美的，因為它們是美的；祢是善的，因為它們是好的；祢是實在的，因為它們存在。

……

【五】祢怎樣創造天地的呢？祢用哪一架機器來進行如此偉大的工程？祢不像人間的工匠，工匠是用一個物體形成另一個物體，依照內心的想法，把想像得到的各種形式加諸於物體——這樣的人的靈魂如不是祢創造的，哪來這種能力？

……這一切都歌頌祢是萬有的創造者。但祢怎樣創造萬有的呢？天主，祢怎樣創造了天地？當然，祢創造天地，不是在天上，也不是在地上，不是在空中，也不是在水中，因為這些都在宇宙之中；祢也不是在宇宙之中創造宇宙，因為在造成宇宙之前，還沒有創造宇宙的場所。祢也不是手中拿著什麼工具來創造天地，因為這種不由祢創造而被拿去創造其他事物的工具又從哪裡得來的呢？哪一樣存在的東西，不是憑藉祢的實在而

存在？因此祢一言而萬物資始，祢是用祢的「道」——言語——創造萬有。

【六】但祢怎樣說話呢？是否如「有聲來自雲際說：這是我鍾愛的兒子」一樣？這種聲音有開始有終了，字音接二連三地傳遞，至最後歸於沉寂，這顯然是一種受造物體暫時的振動，是為祢服務，傳達祢永恆的意志。肉體的耳朵聽到這一句轉瞬即逝的言語，傳達給內在理智，理智的內在耳朵傾聽你永恆的言語。理智把這一句暫時有聲響的言語和你永恆的無聲的言語：「道」比較，便說：「二者迥乎不同，前者遠不如我，甚至並不存在，因為是轉瞬即逝的，而我的天主的言語是在我之上，永恆不滅的。」如果祢創造天地，是用一響即逝的言語說話，如果祢真的如此創造了天地，那麼在天地之前，就已存在物質的受造物，這受造物暫時振動，才暫時傳播了這些話……

……

【十二】對於提出：「天主創造天地前在做什麼？」這樣的問題的人，我不採用那種打趣式的答語來回答這嚴肅的問題說：「天主正在為放言高論者準備地獄。」看清問題是一回事，打趣是另一回事。我對不知道的事寧願回答說：「不知道」，也不願嘲笑人們的探賾索隱，而以乖誤謬答贏得贊許。

但是，我的天主，我說祢萬有的創造者，如果天地二字指一切受造之物，我敢大膽地說：天主在創造天地之前，不造一物。因為如果造，那麼除了創造受造之物外，能造什麼？巴

不得我能知道我所願知道而且知之有益的一切，猶如我知道在一切受造之物造成之前，別無受造之物。

【十三】……思想膚淺的人徘徊於過去時代的印象中，覺得非常詫異，以為創造一切和掌握一切的全能天主、天地的創造者，在進行如許工程之前，虛度著無量數的世紀而無所事事。我希望他蘇醒過來，認識他的詫異是錯誤的。祢既然是一切時間的創造者，在祢未造時間之前，怎能有無量數的世紀過去？能有不經祢建定的時間嗎？時間既不存在，何謂過去？既然祢是一切時間的創造者，假定在祢創造天地之前，有時間存在，怎能說祢無所事事呢？這時間既然是祢創造的，在祢創造時間之前，就沒有分秒時間能過去。如果在天地之前沒有時間，為何要問在「那時候」祢做什麼？沒有時間，便沒有所謂「那時候」。

祢不是在時間上超越時間：否則祢就不能超越一切時間了。祢是在永永現在的永恆高峰上超越一切過去，也超越一切將來，因為將來的，來到後即成過去；「祢永不改變，祢的歲月沒有窮盡」。祢的歲月既不來亦不往，我們的歲月卻既來亦往，都在遞延之中。祢的歲月全部屹立著絕不過去，不被將來者推排而去，而我們的歲月過去便了。祢是「千年如一日」，祢的日子，沒有每天，只有今天，因為祢的今天既不遞嬗與明天，也不繼承著昨天。祢的今天即是永恆。祢生了同屬永恆的一位，祢對祂說：「我今日生祢」。祢創造了一切時間，祢在一切時間之前。而非沒有時間存在之前有某一段時間。

【十四】……時間究竟是什麼？誰能簡易概括地說明它？誰能對此有明確的思想概念，能用言語表達出來？可是在日常談話之中，有什麼比時間更常見，更熟悉呢？我們談到時間，當然了解，聽別人談到時間，我們也領會。那麼時間究竟是什麼？沒有人問我，我倒清楚，有人問我，我想說明，反倒茫然不解了。但我敢自信地說，如果沒有事物消逝，即沒有過去的時間；沒有事物生成，也就沒有將來的時間，並且如果什麼也不存在，則也沒有現在的時間。既然過去已經不在，將來尚未來到，則過去和將來這兩個時間怎樣存在呢？現在如果永久是現在，便沒有時間，而是永恆。現在之所以成為時間，乃由於走向過去；那麼我們怎能說現在存在呢？現在所以在的原因是即將不在；因此，除非時間走向不存在，否則我便不能正確地說時間存在。

　　……

【二十四】……物體運動時，我用時間來度量物體從開始運動至停止共歷多少時間。如果我沒有看見運動的開始，以及運動持續不輟，那也就看不到它的停止，我便無法度量，而只能估計我從看見到看不見所歷的時間。如果我看見的時間很久，也只能說時間很長，而無法確定多少時間。如要確定多少時間，就必須作出比較，譬如說：彼此一樣，彼此相差一倍，或諸如此類的關係。

　　……既然物體的運動是一件事，估計運動歷時多少是另一件事，那麼誰會看不出二者之中哪一樣應名為時間？各種

物體有時活動，有時靜止，我們不僅估計活動的時間，也估計靜止的時間，我們說：「靜止和活動的時間相等」，或「靜止的時間為活動時間的一倍或兩倍」，或作其他定斷，或作所謂近似的估計。所以時間並非物體的運動。

……

【二十七】……我的心靈啊，我是在你裡面度量時間。不要否定我的話，事實是如此。也不要在印象的波浪之中否定你自己。我再說一次，我是在你裡面度量時間片段。事物經過時，在你裡面留下印象，事物過去而印象留著。我是度量現在的知覺而不是度量激起它而已經過去的實質；我度量時間的時候，是度量印象。為此，或者印象即是時間，或者我所度量的仍並非時間。

問題討論：

1. 奧古斯丁從受造物是「美的」、「善的」與「實存的」，就直接推論到創造萬物的上帝也是「美的」、「善的」與「實存的」，這樣的推論有沒有問題？

2. 奧古斯丁說：「現在之所以成為時間，乃由於走向過去；那麼我們怎能說現在存在呢？現在所以在的原因是即將不在；因此，除非時間走向不存在，否則我便不能正確地說時間存在。」這樣的推論您認為正確嗎？

3. 奧古斯丁利用印象的記憶、感覺與預期，來說明時間的過去、現在與未來，這種想法是否可靠？譬如我們突然進入某種似曾相識的場景，眼前的現在感覺，似乎我在過去就曾經遭遇，也就是「我曾在過去遭遇到未來的眼前這一刻」，這似乎證明現在的「感覺」其實有可能被列為「過去」已發生且又在過去的「未來」（也就是現在）中重現為同一事件，因此現在的「感覺」是不是一定被認為是「現在」而不會是「過去」或「未來」？

延伸閱讀：

1. Saint Augustine, *Confessions* (tr. Henry Chadwick), Oxford University Press, 1991.

2. 周偉馳著，《奧古斯丁的基督教思想》，北京，中國社會科學出版社，2005 年。

七、笛卡兒——我思故我在

王志銘

單元旨要：

　　法國開啟近代哲學發展最重要的哲學家，號稱「近代哲學之父」的笛卡兒 (René Descartes A. C., 1596 –1650)，母親早逝父再娶，由祖母與乳母養大。年輕時曾投身軍旅，但興趣卻在數學與科學理論的研究，最重要的成就是把代數與幾何學結合而完成近代數學的根基「解析幾何」，為近代高等數學開啟了研究的大門，故又被尊稱為「近代數學之父」，我們今天能夠利用數學運算精準地預測與掌握人造衛星或太空梭的飛行軌跡，可以說全拜笛卡兒之賜。1630 年起隱居荷蘭寫作，十八年間不斷更換住處。1633 年聽聞伽利略被審定罪後，更不敢將支持哥白尼地動說的物理學方面著作公諸於世。1635 年與女僕生下一個女兒，但就在笛卡兒出版劃時代巨著《沉思錄》之前病逝，留給笛卡兒無限的哀痛。1649 年應瑞典女王之邀前往斯德哥爾摩講學，不幸感染肺炎，死於 1650 年。

　　笛卡兒在方法論上提出了迥異於亞里斯多德三段論邏輯的體系，並列出科學研究四個重要規箴：

1. 懷疑：如果不清不楚，而有可能被質疑，就不要當真。
2. 分析：把困難的問題分為多個簡單的部分個別解決。
3. 建構：從個別簡單的進一步到複雜困難的。
4. 再審：經常檢查，是否探索過程能臻完善。

　　可惜這樣的方法論在物理科學方面並沒有為他帶來更大的成就，由於太重視「分析」而忽略實驗歸納的重要，科學方面的成就反而被後來居上的牛頓等人所掩蓋。但這個方法論卻在哲學的形而上學領域發揮了它的長處，笛卡兒在拋棄了無法信任的感覺領域之後，轉而在精神性的思想自身找到了可靠不容懷疑的知識根基。類似於奧古斯丁所言的「當我們懷疑，這個懷疑本身就不容再被懷疑」，笛卡兒進一步從這裡確立「當我正在懷疑，也就是正在思考的時候，這個思想著的我就不容再被懷疑」，換句話說「我思考，所以我存在」，這是最不容被懷疑而作為一切確定知識基礎的根底。笛卡兒在《沉思錄》中設想自己有可能被一個強大的魔鬼所掌控，人類一切思緒感覺亦都被這魔鬼所控制，以至於眼前所想所見都不過是這魔鬼操控的結果而不是真實，因此萬事萬物乃至我們覺得非常真實的身體，都有可能只是幻象或夢境而已。可是正當我們在思想中出現懷疑的時候，「有這懷疑」乃至「有這懷疑的思想」本身卻又是千真萬確不容被懷疑的，換句話說魔鬼如果想要欺騙我，首先他就必須讓這有所思的「我」成為千真萬確的事實。笛卡兒就利用這一不容再被質疑的「思想我」，進一步確立這一「思想我」中所確信的數學命題、幾何形狀乃至「完滿至善的上帝」等概念也都是先天上必然為真的，並由至善的上帝推論出，上帝讓我們看見聽見的這個物理世界也必然是真實的。

　　儘管笛卡兒《沉思錄》所使用的這套思想方法，後來遭受諸多大哲學家的質疑，但無可否認的事實是，沒有笛卡兒打開這一個思想大門，就沒有後續的諸多哲學家能夠毫無憑據地競相跳脫中世紀以來亞里斯多德主義的掌控。英國的經驗主義大師大衛・休姆 (David Hume) 後來就質疑「思想我」也仍不過是一束知覺透過想像力綑綁在一起的幻想而已。而德國的伊曼紐・康德 (Immanuel Kant) 儘管反對笛卡兒唯心論的實體主

義與大衛・休姆的懷疑主義，但也把「自我意識的統一性」當作人類經驗成立的先驗條件，這何嘗不是起源於笛卡兒思想的激發？至於德國唯心論企圖從心靈活動進而推導出整個實體世界的開展，內容也許與笛卡兒不盡相同，路數卻不可否認地更貼近於笛卡兒的思想方法。

現代的大腦科學，固然證實了笛卡兒將心靈擺在大腦中心的「松果腺」是一個錯誤的推測，但卻也證實了像顏色、聲音甚至形狀這些現象的確是神經系統受到外界刺激（笛卡兒稱之為撞擊）後，由大腦神經利用先天既有的處理系統主動形成的知覺結果。心靈固然在運作上離不開大腦神經系統，但科學家也還不敢武斷地將心靈等同於這些湊在一塊的神經細胞，時至今日笛卡兒的心物二元論，在哲學領域內也還是有一定的市場支持度。

下面這段文本採自笛卡兒晚期 1644 年出版的《哲學原理》第一卷，內容簡明扼要地概述了「我思故我在」的思路，雖然沒有《沉思錄》來得複雜詳盡，但所陳述的思想卻是一貫的。

選讀文本：

1. 要想追求真理，我們必須在一生中盡可能地把所有事物都懷疑一次。既然我們曾經一度是兒童，在我們還不能完全運用理性之時，就已經對感官所見的物件，構成了各種判斷，因而就有許許多多的偏見阻礙了我們認識真理的道路；我們如果不把自己覺得有點可疑的事物，在一生中至少加以懷疑一次，我們似乎就不可能排除掉這些既有的偏見。

2. 凡可被懷疑的事物，我們也都應當認為是虛妄不實的。另外，如果把我們可能懷疑的事物也都假設是虛妄的，那也是有益的。這樣，我們就可以更加明白地發現具有最大確定性和最易明白認識的真理。

......

4. 我們為什麼懷疑可感的事物。既然我們現在只打算從事研究真理，我們首先就要懷疑：落於我們感官之前的一切事物，和我們所想像的一切事物，其中是否有一種是真正實在的？我們所以如此懷疑，第一，根據經驗，各種感官有時是會犯錯的，如果過度信賴曾經欺騙過我們的感官，那就是魯莽草率的。第二，在夢中我們雖然不斷地想像或知覺到無數的物象，可是它們實際上並不存在。一個人如果決心懷疑一切，就看不到什麼標記，可以用來精確地分辨睡眠和覺醒的狀態。

5. 此外我們為什麼還要懷疑我們一向認為最確定的其他事物，甚至於要懷疑數學的解證，以及我們一向認為自明的那些原理？我們所以要懷疑，第一，因為我們曾經看見人們在這些事情上面犯過許多錯誤，而

且把我們認為虛妄的事物認為是絕對確定而自明的。不過主要的原因仍在：我們知道創造我們的那位上帝是全能的，但我們卻還不知道，上帝是否有意把我們這樣創造出來，使我們即使在自己認為最熟悉的事物方面也永遠受到欺騙。我們的觀察既然告訴我們，我們有時是要受騙的，那麼我們為什麼不能永久受騙呢？如果我們認為全能的上帝不是我們人類的創造者，而認為我們是自己存在的，或以其他方法存在的，那麼，我們越是認為自己的創造者沒有權力，我們就越有理由相信我們並不十分完美以至不會繼續受騙。

......

7. 我們在懷疑時，不能懷疑自己的存在，而且在我們依次推論時，這就是我們所得到的第一種知識。我們既然排斥了稍可懷疑的一切事物，甚至想像它們是虛妄的，那麼我們的確很容易假設，既沒有上帝，也沒有蒼天，也沒有物體；也很容易假設我們自己甚至沒有手沒有腳，最後竟沒有身體。不過我們在懷疑這些事物的真實性時，我們卻不能同樣假設我們是不存在的。因為要想像一種有思想呈現的東西是不存在的，那就會是一種自相矛盾。因此，我思故我在的這種知識，乃是一個有條理進行推論的人所體會到的最先的、最確定的知識。

8. 我們於此就能發現心靈和身體的區別，或能思的事物和物質的事物的分別。這就是發現心靈本質的最好方法，也就是發現心靈與身體的差異的最好方法。既然我們假設除了思想以外，沒有別的事物真正存在，那麼，我們在考察自己的本來面目時，就分明看到，凡身體所具有的廣袤、形相、位置的移動，以及其他相似情節，都不屬於我們的本性──只有思想除外。因此，我們對自己的心靈所具有的意念，

是在我們對任何物質事物所具有的意念以前存在的，而且是較為確定的，因為我們在已經知道自己是在思想時，我們仍然在懷疑有任何身體存在。

9. 思想 (cogitatio) 是什麼。所謂思想，就是在我們身上發生而為我們所直接意識到的一切，因此，不只是理解 (intelligere, entendre)、意欲 (velle)、想像 (imaginari)，就是知覺 (sentire, sentir)，也和思想 (cogitare, penser) 無異。如果我在說話、看物、行走時，依靠視覺和走路了解我的眼睛或腿的動作（這些都是身體的動作）就認為我是存在的，那麼這個結論就並不是絕對正確的。因為，正如在夢中那樣，我雖不會張眼或移動位置，甚至也許沒有身體，可是我也可以設想自己在看物或行走。但是，如果我只是指感覺本身，或對於視或行的那種意識本身，那麼這種知識分明是確定的，因為這只是就心靈來說的，而只有心靈才能知覺或意識到自己的視或行的動作。

10. ……「我思故我在」的這個命題，是最基本、最確定的。……

問題討論：

1. 從「我正在思考」，真的就能推論出「我存在」嗎？那如果一個機器人被設計成能夠思索「我正在思考」，那這機器人就跟人一樣，擁有一個不容被懷疑而且迥異於機械物體的「心靈」囉？

2. 從一個各部分皆為真的簡單命題，組合出來的複雜命題必然也是「真」的嗎？例如：上一刻的「思想我」為真，下一刻的「思想我」也為真，再加上這一刻的「思想我」也為真，就能得出一個複雜命題「所有時刻裡都有一個思想我，而且是同一個我」也是真的嗎？

3. 除了上述兩個問題之外，您能嘗試就上面的文本，自己提出一個不同的問題嗎？

延伸閱讀：

1. Tom Sorell, *Descartes: A Very Short Introduction*, Oxford University Press, 2000.

2. 笛卡兒著，周春塘譯，《沉思錄》，臺北，五南圖書，2010 年。

八、康德——論經驗的界限

王志銘

單元旨要：

德國最偉大的哲學家伊曼紐·康德 (Immanuel Kant)，1724 年生於 Königsberg（今天立陶宛的 Kaliningrad），一個窮困的馬具製造匠家庭，父母為路德宗虔敬派 (Pietism) 教徒，強調良心是引導人行為的最高權威。八歲進入虔敬派學校寄讀，過著極嚴苛的紀律生活。三十一歲當上大學私人教師，陸續講授形上學與邏輯，四十六歲當上正教授，五十六歲出版劃時代巨作：《純粹理性批判》，開啟了德國哲學的黃金時代。

康德的日常生活相當刻板，每天五點起床備課至七點，上完早課後繼續寫作讀書至下午一點，用過一天唯一的一餐之後，不管晴雨一定單獨出外散步，據說成為當地婦女校正時鐘的依據。唯一一次破壞生活常軌，是因貪讀盧梭著作《愛彌兒》而忘了作息。1792 年因撰寫《純粹理性界限內的宗教》一書而觸怒當局，差點被捕。隔年菲特烈二世去世才出版。

終身未娶。1804 年辭世。墓誌銘上刻著：「仰觀天上無數星斗，俯視內心中的諸多道德法則，這兩樣東西，每當我深沉靜思，就越發令我感到驚歎與敬畏！」

直到今日，德國人對康德的敬重就像中國人之於孔子。

　　康德的思想主要在於回答下列三個問題：

1. 我能夠知道什麼？

　　代表歐洲大陸理性論思潮的萊布尼茲，宣稱我們可以擁有不受任何觀察者個人經驗污染的關於這個世界的客觀知識。相反地，英國海島的經驗論者大衛・休謨，則認為一切知識都來自於經驗，他甚至否定笛卡兒認為不證自明的自我意識及理性論強調的因果關係，認為這些都不過是人類心靈幻想的產物而已。康德先是支持理性論的觀點，後來受到大衛・休謨因果思想的衝擊，放棄了原來理性論的立場，並花了將近十年的工夫，發展出一套調和理性論與經驗論的批判哲學，他強調：經驗的感性直觀，若沒有理性概念的介入，將只是一團混亂的雜多而已；反之，理性概念若沒有經驗內容做它的對象，就只會陷入盲目的亂想。康德認為一切客觀經驗，都藉由理性的概念範疇才成為可能；但也因此，這些先天概念的使用範圍就只能限定在經驗界限之內，一旦超出經驗範圍去使用，就只會陷入無解的矛盾命題之中。譬如：我們可以使用「量」範疇去說明站在我們眼前是一個人或三個人。但如果我們超越經驗界限去使用這種範疇，我們就會陷入自我矛盾無法解決，例如基督教一直爭論不休的問題：聖父聖子聖靈究竟是一位還是三位？

　　因此，他得到了一個劃時代的結論：物自體不可知，我們所能知道的不過就是經驗界內的現象。

　　那麼大家都喜歡談論的宗教信仰，尤其是西方基督教信仰的「上帝存在」或「靈魂不朽」等等形上學命題又該如何處理呢？

　　當純粹運用在經驗世界的理論理性在形上學思考歷程走不下去時，康德想到了人還有實踐理性。於是他接著問：

2. 我應該做什麼？

　　西方倫理自亞里斯多德提出「幸福」作為最高的目標之後，這種以幸福結果作為行為道德判斷依據的思想整整主宰了西方思想界兩千年，直到康德才有所突破。康德認為人類行為的道德性，在於行為的動機，而不在於行為所能促成的效果。而這個動機就是在於行動時有沒有把自己與他人都當作「目的自身」而不是「工具」來看待，因此道德的最高命令就是：「僅按照你及他人的目的自身都可以同時存在的方式去行動」，這個內在動機形式上又可以被改寫成一個用來判別所有行動準則的無上斷言令式：「僅按照你認為可以成為普遍法則的格律去行動」。只要能通過這一形式檢驗的，就是我們應當去做的義務。

3. 我可以希望什麼？

　　根據上述「為義務而義務」而不是「為幸福而義務」的這種行動理論，康德進一步論述「有德斯有福」這種願望其實常常是落空的。我們的日常經驗裡不乏這種「有道德的人慘遭厄運，不道德的人卻坐擁豪宅美食」的例子。而這種德福不一致的現實狀況卻會削弱道德實踐的意志，因此實踐理性有必要透過一種宗教信仰的方式，要求「上帝存在」與「靈魂不朽」來保證德福一致的必然實現。康德因此建立了一種迥異於過往的道德形上學。

　　下面這篇文章，選自康德《純粹理性批判》第二版的序言，可以說是他整個思想體系的一個縮影，從追問「先天綜合命題如何可能？」翻轉整個思路，既不說知識完全起源於經驗，亦不說知識完全起源於理性，而採取了一種「理性之受教於自然，並非像學生之受教於教師，只聽從教師之所言，而是像受任命的法官，去強迫證人答復法官所提的考問。」的嶄新思維模式，去處理知識的問題。他所論及的先於經驗而運用於經驗的這些人類認知的先天能力，縱使推測不完全精準，但今天的許多認知科學研究，卻證實了這方向基本上是正確而有價值的。至於形而上學的部分，東西方思維未必能夠一致，佛教因果業報一樣可以形成全然不同於西方的靈魂不朽觀念，同樣能滿足善有善報惡有惡報的實踐要求，卻不需要預設一位全知全能的審判者。

選讀文本：

論究屬於理性領域內的知識……

邏輯學自從古代以來，早已進展到穩固的路徑中……直到今日邏輯學已不可能再往前進一步發展，它的外表看來已經是非常完善的學問了……邏輯學的範圍早就已經嚴謹確定了，它的唯一職責，就在：對於一切思維……方式的規律，加以詳盡說明及嚴格證明而已。

邏輯學所以能有這樣的成就，是因為它本身的限制，因此能有正當理由抽掉……知識一切內容物以及物與物的所有差別，而僅僅論究所留存於悟性自身的思考形式……

數學在人類理性史可及範圍內，早就藉由希臘這偉大的民族進入堅實的途徑……亦即早已在論證二等邊三角形性質的第一個人……心中顯露。數學所創立的真正方法，不在於檢驗圖形中或圖形概念中所涉及的事物，以及理解事物性質；而在於發現數學必然內含於「先天構成的概念」中……數學若以先天的正確性知道任何事物，則除了必然是由其自身依據自身概念而加入於圖形者之外，絕不附加任何事物。

自然科學進入學問之大道，則為時甚晚……

伽利略 (Galileo)……知曉理性所能洞察的，僅限於理性按其自身之計畫所產生之事物，又知曉理性不容其自身被自然所支配，而是依據固定法則的判斷原理指示著行進的途徑，而強迫著自然來答復理性自身所給定的問題。凡偶然的觀察不遵從理性所預先設定之計畫者，絕

不能夠產出必然法則，但理性卻唯以發見此種必然法則為其任務。理性左執原理……右執實驗……為了要受教於自然，故必接近自然。但理性之受教於自然，並非像學生之受教於教師，只聽從教師之所言，而是像受任命的法官，去強迫證人答復法官所提的考問。

形上學作為全然孤立的理性思辨學問，高翔於經驗教導之外……形上學唯獨根據概念……形上學雖較一切學問為古，設使一切學問被破壞一切的野蠻主義所摧毀，形上學依然能夠存留下來，但形上學實際上尚未幸運地進入學問安穩的途徑，因為在形上學裡……理性常遇到死路，亦無法引領我們邁向想到達的路途，在形上學中吾人其實只是不斷徘徊卻步而已。形上學領域裡的學徒在彼此相互論辯中遠不能展示出一致的成果，因此形上學無寧應特別被視為適合練習武術者的戰場而已，在此戰場中卻沒有一個參與者真正能夠獲得盈寸之地，且亦無法確保能夠永久占有。由此觀之，過往形上學的進展，絕不容疑地僅是在盲目摸索，其尤為惡劣者，則僅僅是在概念中盲目地摸索而已。

……但何以自然又賦與吾人理性從未止歇的努力去探求形上學途徑，好像這就是理性最關切的重要事項……

……我們所有知識必定與事物相一致，這是以往的假定。然而在這種假定的基礎上，單單透過概念就試圖先天地對於概念的對象有所建立的企圖，因而亦即擴大知識的那種企圖，卻終告失敗了。因而必須重新嘗試，假設是事物必須與我們的知識相一致，這樣是否形上學會比先前的假定會更有所成……於是我們的進路正好如同哥白尼 (Copernicus) 的假設一樣。當「一切天體圍繞觀察者旋轉」的假設，不

能說明天體運動時，反過來假設是觀察者在旋轉，而星體則是靜止不動的，哥白尼以此成功解釋了天體運動。關於事物的直觀，這同樣的嘗試，也能在形上學中被使用。因為如果直觀必須與事物的性質相合，則我實在不解我們何以能先天地對事物有所認知？反之，如果事物（即感官之事物）必須與吾人直觀能力的質性相符合，那麼此種先天認知的可能性就能容易被理解……

在經驗事物授與我之前，此種悟性規律就已存在我之內部，亦即先天地存在著……經驗的一切事物，必然與這些先天的概念相符，且必須與之相一致……

這種新觀點足以說明何以我們能有先天的知識；而且能夠說明作為經驗對象總合的自然之一切先天基礎法則……但關於先天的認知能力的此種演繹，在形上學第一部分中，雖然具有驚人的效果，但在第二部分中卻與形上學的全部目的，大相逕庭。因為超越了一切經驗界限，雖然這是形上學所唯一企求的，吾人所斷言的，卻是吾人經驗絕不能超越的限界……

迫使吾人超越經驗及一切現象界限的，乃是無條件者，這是理性為了完成條件系列必然而且正當地對於物自身所要求的……超感官領域中，當思辨的理性不容置喙時，卻尚有吾人所能論究的問題，亦即：在理性的實踐知識中，是否能夠發現資料足以敲定理性所有超驗的無條件者的概念，使我們根據形上學的願望，藉著先天知識，超越一切可能的經驗限界（雖然只是自實踐的觀點而言）？思辨理性至少為此留有餘地，同時思辨理性若不能自行擴大，則必須任由此種餘地空閒，而讓我們自由地藉由理性的實踐資料去占領這餘地……

問題討論：

1. 數學命題如：「直角三角形兩邊的平方和等於斜邊的平方。」或「5+7=12」真的像康德所言，是一種先天綜合命題嗎？還是它們都是可以透過演算規則推演出來的命題呢？

2. 你真的想過而且關切「宇宙的起源」或「萬物的起點」這種「無條件者」的問題嗎？如果沒有，那你就欠缺理性思考嗎？

3. 你有沒有宗教信仰？你的宗教信仰真的是建立在這種「善有善報惡有惡報」的要求上嗎？

延伸閱讀：

1. 康德著，鄧曉芒譯，《純粹理性批判》，臺北，聯經出版社，2004 年。

2. 王志銘，〈道德神學在道德上是必然的嗎？〉國立臺灣大學哲學系，《哲學論評》，第 29 期，2005 年，頁 65-98。

九、穆勒——捍衛個人自由

徐 佐 銘

單元旨要：

目前的臺灣社會，是一個高度「個人主義」(individualism) 及「反威權」(anti-authority) 的時代。年輕世代普遍努力掙脫父母與師長的嚴厲管教，擺脫傳統禮教的束縛，反抗國家與政府的不當管制，嚮往自由自在的個人生活。

在這個單元的經典導讀裡，我們要一起閱讀的是英國哲學家約翰・司圖亞特・穆勒 (John Stuart Mill, 1806-1873) 在 1859 年出版的書《論自由》(*On Liberty*)。穆勒這本書不但散發出濃郁的「個人主義」色彩，同時也贏得「自由主義」(liberalism) 開山祖師的崇高地位。對於熱烈追求個人自由的當代人而言，這本經典不但沒有過時，而且還歷久彌新。

在選讀文本 1. 裡，穆勒聲明他這本論文的主題不是「意志自由」，而是「公民自由」或稱「社會自由」。而所謂社會自由的議題是：社會合法運用它的力量施加於個人身上的本質是什麼？限制是什麼？這段暗示，社會不可以濫用它的力量施加於個人身上，亦即，社會應受到某些限制。

在選讀文本 2. 裡，穆勒指出，所謂的「自我管理」，在實際的情況中，並非每個個人自己管理自己，而是握有力量的「多數人」在管理其餘的

人。由於多數人可能想去壓制其他的社會成員，因此預防這種事情的發生，正如預防社會力量的濫用一樣重要。

在選讀文本 3. 裡，穆勒提到「多數專制」主要訴諸社會威權去運作。

綜合以上三個選文，再考察 19 世紀的英國以及 21 世紀當代情形，我們就會更加了解深義。1859 年《論自由》出版的年代，英國已是歐洲當時相當進步的君主立憲國家。儘管仍有維多利亞女王，但她並非柏拉圖所嚮往的「哲學王」。「國會議員多數決」已取代古代君主的「獨裁」。在邁向越來越成熟的「民主政治」體制的過程中，穆勒很有遠見地預見當代 21 世紀民主國家「多數專制」的弊病。簡言之，在多數決的民主體制下，少數族群有可能遭受多數族群的壓制或歧視。一旦遭受不平等待遇時，少數族群想要「要回」被剝奪的權利時，往往會遭受「多數專制」的阻撓。以美國同性婚姻合法化為例，同性戀者「要回」本該享有卻被剝奪的合法婚姻權，仍然要歷經數十年的努力，等到「過半」民意的支持，以及最高法院九位法官 5:4 多數同意，才爭取到婚姻合法。

相較於歐盟許多國家，美國直到 2015 年 6 月 26 日才通過同性婚姻合法，可說落後不少。至於臺灣，進展更慢。2014 年 12 月 22 日，立法院司法及法制委員會首度審查同性婚姻時，與會人士都知道，民意調查顯示，關於同性婚姻，55% 贊成，37% 反對。儘管如此，接受質詢的法務部次長陳明堂仍表示反對，理由是「尚未達成共識」、「破壞現有婚姻制度」及「造成社會動盪」。

　　試觀選讀文本 4. 和 5.，穆勒提出兩個重要主張：(1) 個人的行為不應傷害到他人；(2) 如果個人的行為沒有傷害到他人的話，社會無權干涉個人的行為。這是自由主義的傳統主張，但有時 (1) 被反對者加以扭曲，(2) 則被忽視。

　　關於 (1) 被扭曲，有一種反對論述是，認為自由主義主張「只要我喜歡，有什麼不可以？」這是一種「稻草人的謬誤」，因為這並非自由主義的主張。事實上，穆勒的目標是「劃定公私領域的界線」，為個人爭取更多不受國家、政府、社會或他人干涉的個人自由。為了捍衛個人自由，(1) 是必要且合理的主張。

　　至於 (2)，雖然常被忽視，然而在一個民主社會裡，透過理性溝通，我們確實看到，所謂的「多數尊重少數」也有可能實現。同性婚姻合法化的支持者認為，同性婚姻的合法化，不但不是危害婚姻制度，而是再度鞏固婚姻的價值。異性婚姻的合法化絲毫未受損，只不過根據平等原則，擴大了婚姻合法的適用對象。支持者認為，既然婚姻是基本人權，而婚姻制度是社會穩定的重要基石，那麼，同性婚姻的合法化，不但合乎人權，也會使得社會更加穩定。

　　在選讀文本 6.、7.、8. 裡，穆勒極力捍衛個人的言論自由。許多主張言論自由或新聞自由的論述，往往也是受到《論自由》的啟蒙與鼓舞。在 21 世紀，當個人的言論被壓制時，其原因可能是「新聞檢查」，也可能是「學術霸權」。穆勒提醒大家，某個被壓制的言論有可能是真理；反之，我們信以為真的意見可能是錯誤的。我們可能立刻想起哥白尼地球繞太陽運轉的主張，以及他所受到的言論壓制。在今日社會裡，批評他人的言論，有時會構成毀謗而被法律制裁。

在選讀文本 9. 裡，穆勒討論了生活方式、個別差異與人生幸福的重要關聯，這是「多元價值」(pluralism) 與尊重「差異」(variety or difference) 的支持者，所常引用的觀點。穆勒在論述擺脫傳統與教條的生活方式時，散發出鮮明的「個人主義」。他相信，當個人追求他自己的人生幸福時，也會促進社會的進步。

《論自由》一書強力捍衛個人的自由，聲援被壓制的少數族群，使得自由主義向來都是解放運動的掛帥理論。同樣是解放派，同樣是聲援被壓制的族群，自由主義卻遭受馬克思「左派解放」的猛烈批評，而被歸類為「右派解放」。左派解放認為自由主義由於忽略了社會結構上的壓迫，因而解放不夠徹底。

選讀文本：

1. The subject of this Essay is not the so-called Liberty of the Will, so unfortunately opposed to the misnamed doctrine of Philosophical Necessity; but Civil, or Social Liberty: the nature and limits of the power which can be legitimately exercised by society over the individual.

2. It was now perceived that such phrases as "self-government", and "the power of the people over themselves", do not express the true state of the case. The "people" who exercise the power are not always the same people with those over whom it is exercised; and the "self-government" spoken of is not the government of each by himself, but of each by all the rest. The will of the people, moreover, practically means the will of the most numerous or the most active part of the people; the majority, or those who succeed in making themselves accepted as the majority; the people, consequently, may desire to oppress a part of their number; and precautions are as much needed against this as against any other abuse of power.

3. Like other tyrannies, the tyranny of the majority was at first, and is still vulgarly, held in dread, chiefly as operating through the acts of the public authorities.

4. That the only purpose for which power can be rightfully exercised over any member of a civilized community, against his will, is to prevent harm to others.

5. The only part of the conduct of any one, for which he is amenable to society, is that which concerns others. In the part which merely concerns himself, his independence is, of right, absolute. Over himself, over his own body and mind, the individual is sovereign.

6. It is necessary to consider separately these two hypotheses, each of which has a distinct branch of the argument corresponding to it. We can never be sure that the opinion we are endeavouring to stifle is a false opinion; and if we were sure, stifling it would be an evil still.

7. First: the opinion which it is attempted to suppress by authority may possibly be true. Those who desire to suppress it, of course deny its truth; but they are not infallible. They have no authority to decide the question for all mankind, and exclude every other person from the means of judging. To refuse a hearing to an opinion, because they are sure that it is false, is to assume that their certainty is the same thing as absolute certainty. All silencing of discussion is an assumption of infallibility.

8. Let us now pass to the second division of the argument, and dismissing the supposition that any of the received opinions may be false, let us assume them to be true, and examine into the worth of the manner in which they are likely to be held, when their truth is not freely and openly canvassed. However unwillingly, a person who has a strong opinion may admit the possibility that his opinion may be false, he ought to be moved by the consideration that however true it may be, if it is not fully, frequently, and fearlessly discussed, it will be held as a dead dogma, not a living truth.

9. As it is useful that while mankind are imperfect there should be different opinions, so is it that there should be different experiments of living; that free scope should be given to varieties of character, short of injury to others; and that the worth of different modes of life should be proved practically, when any one thinks fit to try them. It is desirable, in short, that in things which do not primarily concern others, individuality should assert itself. Where, not the person's own character, but the traditions or customs of other people are the rule of conduct, there is wanting one of the principal ingredients of human happiness, and quite the chief ingredient of individual and social progress.

問題討論：

1. 以上九段選文當中，哪一段或哪幾段最深得你意？嘗試聯結到自己的生活。

2. 以上九段選文當中，哪一段或哪幾段你有不同的意見？試提出你的評論。

3. 哪些個人的言論應讓它發表，不受干涉？哪些言論應該禁止發表？舉例說明。

4. 關於同性婚姻合法化，你有什麼主張或看法？

延伸閱讀：

1. Isaiah Berlin 著，陳曉林譯，《自由四論》，臺北，聯經出版社，1986 年。

2. 《立法院公報》，第 104 卷第 5 期（2014 年 12 月 22 日，司法及法制）委員會紀錄，2014 年。

3. Adam Liptak, "Supreme Court Ruling Makes Same-Sex Marriage a Right Nationwide", *The New York Times*, June 26, 2015.

4. 鄭光明，《我的自由，不自由？——10 則青春校園的哲學激辯》，臺北，三民書局，2015 年。

十、孔子論「三年之喪」── 良知與效益

鄭鈞瑋

單元旨要：

　　《論語》是重要的儒家哲學經典。今天我們看到的通行本《論語》，共二十篇，每篇若干章，取篇首二到三字為篇名，共四百九十二章，內容主要是記錄孔子及其弟子的言行。本段文字選自〈陽貨〉篇，與《論語》其他篇章不同的是，其他篇章大多為孔子單向式申述主張或直接回應問題，而此處卻難得地呈現了孔子和其弟子宰我，針對「三年之喪」這個議題針鋒相對的論辯。透過他們的論證和思想交鋒，反而能讓我們更深入的理解孔子的哲學主張。並且，經由此番討論與對話，更能幫助我們理解孔子的核心思想──「仁」。因此，不少學者認為本章是《論語》全書中相當關鍵的一章。

　　本段選文中，宰我質疑「三年之喪」的合理性，認為守喪一年已經足夠了。宰我的立基點兼顧人文秩序與自然秩序。他提出的理由有兩點：一是認為如此將造成禮壞樂崩的結果，反使人文價值崩壞；二是認為自然界運行的規律也是一年為一個循環。因此，守喪三年時間太長了，是不合理的。孔子則認為宰我忽視了人內心的真誠感受，忽略了倫理規範最核心的根源乃是人的真情實感，因此責備宰我「不仁」。針對宰我，孔子也提出了兩個理由。首先，針對宰我訴諸經驗界自然規律，孔子也訴諸子女至少需要父母養育三年這項經驗事實，認為報答父母養育之恩是人性中普遍

的情感要求。第二，針對宰我訴諸人文秩序，孔子則是訴諸文化傳統和共通人性，認為「三年之喪」符合人文秩序，乃是天下普遍施行的制度。

如果我們不拘泥在「三年之喪」這個特定議題上，進一步來看孔子與宰我論辯中蘊含的哲學思考，會發現他們爭論的焦點在於「制度或行為的合理性是基於什麼」。宰我主要認為要由「實際效果」來論斷制度是否合理。因此，若遵守某一制度卻產生負面的結果，則此制度就是不合理的。而孔子則認為要判別制度是否合理是依據人的「良心或道德直覺」。所以，若某制度讓人覺得良心不安則表示此制度有問題。

本段文字亦在倫理學上呈現了儒家哲學傳統有別於西方哲學傳統的特色。從蘇格拉底開始，西方哲學傳統主要將道德立基於理性思辯上，判斷行為對錯的關鍵因素在於這個行為是不是能夠經得起理性的檢證。能夠合理化的便是對的行為；不能合理化的則是錯誤的行為。至於以哪方面作為檢證的判準，則又產生以「行為所產生的結果」來判斷，抑或是以「行為本身的特質」來判斷這兩大派別。儒家哲學對道德的思考進路則有異於是。從孔子對宰我的回答可以看出，孔子認為判斷行為對錯的關鍵因素是人的真情實感。符合人真誠感受的，便是對的行為；違背人真情實感的，便是無法被認同的行為。因此，在〈子路〉篇中，對於檢舉父親偷羊的行為，孔子便無法認同。

以下，讓我們一起閱讀這份哲學經典吧！跟著孔子和宰我的討論，一起來思考道德和我們日常生活的關係吧！

選讀文本：

1. 宰我問：「三年之喪，期已久矣。君子三年不為禮，禮必壞；三年不為樂，樂必崩。舊穀既沒，新穀既升，鑽燧改火，期可已矣。」子曰：「食夫稻，衣夫錦，於女安乎？」曰：「安。」「女安則為之！夫君子之居喪，食旨不甘，聞樂不樂，居處不安，故不為也。今女安，則為之！」宰我出。子曰：「予之不仁也！子生三年，然後免於父母之懷。夫三年之喪，天下之通喪也。予也有三年之愛於其父母乎？」《論語・陽貨》

2. 葉公語孔子曰：「吾黨有直躬者，其父攘羊，而子證之。」孔子曰：「吾黨之直者異於是。父為子隱，子為父隱，直在其中矣。」《論語・子路》

問題討論：

1. 關於孔子和宰我對於「三年之喪」的討論，你覺得孔子和宰我誰的說法比較有道理？為什麼？

2. 你覺得雙方的論點是否有什麼優缺點？又該如何彌補呢？

3. 你怎麼理解「子為父隱，父為子隱」這句話呢？如果你的親人犯罪了，你是否會站出來檢舉他呢？為什麼？

延伸閱讀：

1. 馮友蘭，《中國哲學史新編·第一冊》，臺北，藍燈文化事業股份有限公司，1991 年，頁 143-147。

2. 勞思光，《新編中國哲學史（一）》，臺北，三民書局，1991 年，頁 127-130、144-145。

3. 李澤厚，《中國古代思想史論》，北京，人民出版社，1985 年，頁 20-21。

4. 林義正，《孔子學說探微》，臺北，東大圖書，1987 年，頁 125-144。

十一、《老子》論仁義—— 自然與人為

鄭鈞瑋

單元旨要：

　　《老子》，又名《道德經》，是道家哲學的重要經典。今天我們看到的通行本《老子》，是魏晉時代哲學家王弼注解整理的版本。王弼本《老子》，共八十一章，分成上下兩篇，上篇從第一章至第三十七章，稱作〈道經〉；下篇則從第三十八章至第八十一章，稱為〈德經〉，因而合稱為《道德經》。除了最為通行的王弼本之外，1973 年於湖南長沙馬王堆漢墓出土的帛書甲本和乙本，以及 1993 年在湖北荊門市郭店楚墓出土的竹簡本，近幾年來也引發了學者廣泛的關注。不同版本間的文字差異與編排次序的不同，當然或多或少會影響我們對《老子》思想的解讀。選文出自最為通行的王弼版本，聚焦於經典的閱讀與哲學議題的討論。

　　一般學界對於《老子》的理解，大多認為《老子》一書中所呈現出的價值取向，乃是對於質樸的肯定以及對於仁義的否定。《老子》第十九章不是明白寫到「絕仁棄義，民復孝慈」嗎？第十八章不是說「大道廢，有仁義」嗎？然而，隨著郭店竹簡的出土，上述主流觀點遭受到了一定程度的挑戰。由於相應於通行本《老子》第十九章的竹簡本，是寫作「絕偽棄慮，民復孝慈」，當中並不涉及任何否定仁義的字眼，因此《老子》對於仁義的觀點又重新引起了討論。《老子》真的反對仁義

嗎？那些看似明顯反對仁義的文字，是否容許做其他解讀呢？讓我們仔細閱讀原文，一起來思考吧！

如果《老子》這些段落確實是在反對仁義，那麼《老子》反對的是仁和義的哪些面向呢？又是根據什麼理由來證成他的主張呢？我們知道，仁和義是儒家哲學中十分推崇的道德價值。仁是真情實感的展現；義是考量對方感受與社會期許所做出的合宜行為。儒家認為統治者推行以仁義為核心的德政，才能使社會和諧；君子以仁義為核心精進修養，方能實現人生命的價值。《老子》哲學崇尚的則是自然與無為。自然指的是不憑藉外力自己如此；無為則是不妄為、不刻意造作。一般所謂的仁義，在《老子》看來，要嘛是統治者刻意的強行作為，要嘛是君子矯揉造作的自我約束，都背離甚至破壞了人原初的質樸，造成各種虛偽狡詐與盲目地競逐標榜的現象。因此，後天才附加在質樸之上的仁義，就成了《老子》要反對的對象。《老子》認為，質樸的狀態中人們自然而然的行為都出於真誠，因而自然符合所謂仁義的要求，但他們並沒有自覺自己是在行仁義。棄絕提倡仁義才能讓社會回歸純樸，恢復人的本真，人才能真正展開生命的價值。

藉由《老子》的這些批判反思，讓我們更深入理解仁義等德行的內涵、思索道德實踐與生命意義的關聯，並進一步反省道德在社會所扮演的角色。

選讀文本：

1. 天地不仁，以萬物為芻狗。聖人不仁，以百姓為芻狗。天地之間，其猶橐籥乎？虛而不屈，動而愈出。多言數窮，不如守中。〈第五章〉

2. 上善若水。水善利萬物而不爭，處眾人之所惡，故幾於道。居善地，心善淵，與善仁，言善信，正善治，事善能，動善時。夫唯不爭，故無尤。〈第八章〉

3. 大道廢，有仁義；智慧出，有大偽；六親不和，有孝慈；國家昏亂，有忠臣。〈第十八章〉

4. 絕聖棄智，民利百倍；絕仁棄義，民復孝慈；絕巧棄利，盜賊無有；此三者，以為文不足。故令有所屬，見素抱樸，少私寡欲。〈第十九章〉

5. 知其雄，守其雌，為天下谿。為天下谿，常德不離，復歸於嬰兒。知其白，守其黑，為天下式。為天下式，常德不忒，復歸於無極。知其榮，守其辱，為天下谷。為天下谷，常德乃足，復歸於樸。樸散則為器，聖人用之則為官長。故大制不割。〈第二十八章〉

6. 上德不德，是以有德；下德不失德，是以無德；上德無為，而無以為；下德為之，而有以為。上仁為之，而無以為；上義為之，而有以為；上禮為之，而莫之應；則攘臂而扔之。故失道而後德，失德而後仁，失仁而後義，失義而後禮。夫禮者忠信之薄而亂之首，前識者道之華而愚之始。是以大丈夫處其厚，不居其薄；處其實，不居其華。故去彼取此。〈第三十八章〉

問題討論：

1. 通過閱讀原文，你覺得《老子》這些討論仁義的段落，是否有不一致的地方呢？你覺得《老子》真的反對仁義嗎？為什麼？

2. 你是否覺得遵守社會上種種道德原則對你是一種制約或壓迫呢？為什麼？你覺得自然而然的一定比人為的好嗎？為什麼呢？

3. 請思考以下情境：今天在捷運上看到一位孕婦，坐在位置上的小明覺得自己很累，但是意識到對方更需要，經過一番天人交戰，終於勉強自己起身讓座。小花則是向來跟著直覺走，從來就沒思考過讓座的意義，這是她第一次搭乘大眾運輸工具。當天她想都沒想，自然而然就直接起身，也不覺得自己是在做一件好事。請問，你認為這兩個人的行為哪一個比較合於道德呢？為什麼？你覺得沒有道德自覺地從事合於道德的行為，算是道德嗎？為什麼呢？

延伸閱讀：

1. 勞思光，《新編中國哲學史（一）》，臺北，三民書局，1991 年，頁 237-253。

2. 陳鼓應，《老莊新論》，臺北，五南圖書，2007 年，頁 105-126。

3. 劉笑敢，《老子：年代新考與思想新詮》，臺北，三民書局，1997 年，頁 68-107、115-145。

十二、《莊子》論逍遙—— 自由與秩序

鄭 鈞 瑋

單元旨要：

今天我們看到的通行本《莊子》，是西晉時代哲學家郭象注解整理的版本。《莊子》一書，共三十三篇，分為內、外、雜三部分。根據學者們的研究，內篇大致上是莊子本人的著作，而外篇與雜篇雖大多是莊子後學的作品，但也保存了一些莊子本人的思想，以及門人對師說的傳承與發展。整本《莊子》固然非一人一時一地之作，但大體可以視為莊子學派之彙編。整部《莊子》以寓言為主，用說故事的方法將讀者帶入莊子瑰瑋的異想世界，透過隱喻的手法使讀者領悟深層的言外之意。莊子經常以其獨特的生活方式和人生智慧，用生命來寫他的哲學，並以詼諧幽默的文筆，使我們當下轉念，心靈得到慰藉。所以自古以來，許多詩人和藝術家都在《莊子》中找到安身立命之道。

「逍遙」是莊子哲學的核心觀念，歷來引發相當多的哲學論辯。引文選自〈逍遙遊〉，為《莊子》全書第一篇。本篇透過「小大之辯」的層層對比，最後點出了「無用之用」，一種令人心嚮往之、無拘無束的生活方式。文中藉著寓言反省何以現實生活中人們總是無法自由，以及使人不自由的因素到底是什麼。根據《莊子》的考察，使人不自由的原因基本上除了客觀生存處境的限制之外，最主要還是自我侷限，是自己的「心」

造成的。我們應該開放自我的心靈，並且要有努力為之的積厚之功，才能使精神突破一切限制，達到自由自在的逍遙境界。

本篇以寓言為主，帶出對「逍遙」這個議題的哲學反思。「逍遙」，相當於我們現在所說的「自由」。《莊子》以「有待」為出發點，來討論自由的意義。有所倚賴，有所限制，會讓我們感到不自由。依賴與限制的程度越高，越不自由；反之，依賴與限制的程度越低，能由自己掌握的部分就越多，就越自由。然而，人畢竟有其限制性，在天生受限制的層面上，是沒有自由可言的。例如一個天生就失明的人，當然沒有看的自由。故談論人的自由，必須是在人的限制範圍內談的，才有意義。

那麼，在先天既有的限制之下，人還有自由可言嗎？《莊子》認為有的。物理的框架無法突破，但人可以突破價值的框架，即是突破人為自己帶來的限制，也就是「無己、無功、無名」。「小知」者畫地自限，未經反省就直接接受規範，於是形同被規範所限制。《莊子》認為，其實人只要願意，可以突破社會功利思考的主流評價，可以超越僵化固執的是非價值評判。當我的選擇是出自我本身，而不是來自於外在的規範，那麼，我就是自由的。即便是生與死的自然事實，人力雖然無從參與，但人可以改變自己面對生死的態度，打破「悅生惡死」的自然趨向，如此就能「乘天地之正，而御六氣之辯，以遊無窮」，達到「無待」，真正的自由自在。

選讀文本：

〈逍遙遊〉

北冥有魚，其名為鯤。鯤之大，不知其幾千里也。化而為鳥，其名為鵬。鵬之背，不知其幾千里也；怒而飛，其翼若垂天之雲。是鳥也，海運則將徙於南冥。南冥者，天池也。

齊諧者，志怪者也。諧之言曰：「鵬之徙於南冥也，水擊三千里，摶扶搖而上者九萬里，去以六月息者也。」野馬也，塵埃也，生物之以息相吹也。天之蒼蒼，其正色邪？其遠而無所至極邪？其視下也，亦若是則已矣。

且夫水之積也不厚，則其負大舟也無力。覆杯水於坳堂之上，則芥為之舟；置杯焉則膠，水淺而舟大也。風之積也不厚，則其負大翼也無力。故九萬里則風斯在下矣，而後乃今培風；背負青天而莫之夭閼者，而後乃今將圖南。

蜩與學鳩笑之曰：「我決起而飛，槍榆枋而止，時則不至而控於地而已矣，奚以之九萬里而南為？」適莽蒼者，三飡而反，腹猶果然；適百里者，宿舂糧；適千里者，三月聚糧。之二蟲又何知！

小知不及大知，小年不及大年。奚以知其然也？朝菌不知晦朔，蟪蛄不知春秋，此小年也。楚之南有冥靈者，以五百歲為春，五百歲為秋；上古有大椿者，以八千歲為春，八千歲為秋。此大年也。而彭祖乃今以久特聞，眾人匹之，不亦悲乎！

　　湯之問棘也是已。窮髮之北，有冥海者，天池也。有魚焉，其廣數千里，未有知其脩者，其名為鯤。有鳥焉，其名為鵬，背若泰山，翼若垂天之雲，摶扶搖羊角而上者九萬里，絕雲氣，負青天，然後圖南，且適南冥也。斥鴳笑之曰：「彼且奚適也？我騰躍而上，不過數仞而下，翱翔蓬蒿之間，此亦飛之至也，而彼且奚適也？」此小大之辯也。

　　故夫知效一官，行比一鄉，德合一君，而徵一國者，其自視也亦若此矣。而宋榮子猶然笑之。且舉世而譽之而不加勸，舉世而非之而不加沮，定乎內外之分，辯乎榮辱之竟，斯已矣。彼其於世，未數數然也。雖然，猶有未樹也。夫列子御風而行，泠然善也，旬有五日而後反。彼於致福者，未數數然也。此雖免乎行，猶有所待者也。若夫乘天地之正，而御六氣之辯，以遊無窮者，彼且惡乎待哉！故曰：至人無己，神人無功，聖人無名。

　　堯讓天下於許由，曰：「日月出矣，而爝火不息，其於光也，不亦難乎！時雨降矣，而猶浸灌，其於澤也，不亦勞乎！夫子立而天下治，而我猶尸之，吾自視缺然。請致天下。」許由曰：「子治天下，天下既已治也。而我猶代子，吾將為名乎？名者，實之賓也，吾將為賓乎？鷦鷯巢於深林，不過一枝；偃鼠飲河，不過滿腹。歸休乎君，予無所用天下為！庖人雖不治庖，尸祝不越樽俎而代之矣。」……

　　惠子謂莊子曰：「魏王貽我大瓠之種，我樹之成而實五石。以盛水漿，其堅不能自舉也。剖之以為瓢，則瓠落無所容。非不呺然大也，吾為其無用而掊之。」莊子曰：「夫子固拙於用大矣。宋人有善為不龜手之藥者，世世以洴澼絖為事。客聞之，請買其方百金。聚族而謀曰：

『我世世為洴澼絖，不過數金；今一朝而鬻技百金，請與之。』客得之，以說吳王。越有難，吳王使之將。冬，與越人水戰，大敗越人，裂地而封之。能不龜手，一也；或以封，或不免於洴澼絖，則所用之異也。今子有五石之瓠，何不慮以為大樽而浮乎江湖，而憂其瓠落無所容？則夫子猶有蓬之心也夫！」

惠子謂莊子曰：「吾有大樹，人謂之樗。其大本擁腫而不中繩墨，其小枝卷曲而不中規矩。立之塗，匠者不顧。今子之言，大而無用，眾所同去也。」莊子曰：「子獨不見狸狌乎？卑身而伏，以候敖者；東西跳梁，不避高下；中於機辟，死於罔罟。今夫斄牛，其大若垂天之雲。此能為大矣，而不能執鼠。今子有大樹，患其無用，何不樹之於無何有之鄉，廣莫之野，彷徨乎無為其側，逍遙乎寢臥其下。不夭斤斧，物無害者，無所可用，安所困苦哉！」

問題討論：

1. 請仔細閱讀引文，對比「鯤鵬」和「蜩與學鳩」，請問他們有哪些差異呢？你覺得《莊子》的立場是什麼？是肯定「鯤鵬」，否定「蜩與學鳩」嗎？或者兩者皆肯定呢？又或者是兩者皆否定呢？你的理由是什麼？

2. 你覺得自由是什麼？自由需要限制嗎？自由和秩序是否衝突？為什麼？

3. 你覺得是不是依賴的程度越少就越自由呢？你認為完全「無待」是否可以得到幸福？或是有所羈絆反而更值得我們追求呢？為什麼？

延伸閱讀：

1. 方勇，《莊子十日談》，上海，上海辭書出版社，2011 年，頁 21-48。

2. 吳怡，《逍遙的莊子》，臺北，三民書局，2004 年。

3. 劉笑敢，《兩種自由的追求：莊子與沙特》，臺北，正中書局，1994 年。

4. 莊子、穆勒、柏林、梁啟超，《論自由》，香港，商務印書館（香港），2005 年。

十三、《孟子》、《荀子》論人性

王靈康

單元旨要：

　　當我們在道德上判斷一件事或一個人的時候，有時會將原因歸結到人性上；如果說不清具體理由的時候，甚至會說出「人性本善」、「人性本惡」這樣的話，彷彿就此徹底道破了問題根源似的。的確，在我們身處的文化傳統裡，確實對於人性有相關的論述。但是我們可以問，在中國古典哲學的原始脈絡裡這類問題究竟是如何討論的，以及，這些討論涵蓋了「人性」的哪些面向？不同的思想家又各是從什麼角度來看待「人性」？我們平常所謂的「人性」和古代思想家所說的意義完全一致嗎？這些問題必須要回到經典原本的脈絡裡找答案。

　　哲學上一般所討論的「人性」，往往是從人的知識能力與道德特性兩方面來談。在此我們要討論的是人在道德方面的特性。在中國古典哲學裡最早、最完整的論述當屬《孟子》和《荀子》。這兩位哲學家都討論了人的「性」；以下我們將進入文獻脈絡，來觀察耳熟能詳的「性善說」和「性惡說」，原本各自是如何剖析人在道德方面的特徵和傾向。

　　先談《孟子》。相傳孟子本人參與了他傳世鉅著的編纂，首先我們看到了以第三人稱的方式記述孟子「道性善」，並且總是藉著引述理想中的遠古聖王事蹟來彰顯他的學說。先王因為對人有不忍之心，所以能

有遍行天下的仁政；而這種不忍之心是所有人都有的。孟子在此舉了個例子來說明我們每個人都有相同的不忍之心。

　　文章裡說，如果眼前忽然看見一個無辜的稚子即將遭遇危險，所有人都會覺得驚恐且不忍，不覺升起出手相救的念頭。這種念頭並非為了博得名聲或利益的考量，也就是說，不是考量出手相救之後的結果能帶來什麼好處，而就是單純地、直接地覺得不忍，這種不忍的心情稱為惻隱之心。在此並特別強調，沒有惻隱之心就不算人，而具有惻隱之心，算是「仁」這種品德發展的端緒、起點。除了惻隱之心，《孟子》還提出了羞惡之心、辭讓之心、是非之心，分別作為「義」、「禮」、「智」這些品德發展的起點。人，擁有道德的這些起點，就像天生具有四肢那麼自然。只要能夠擴充，也就是以這些起點為基礎，就像火苗開始燃燒、又像泉水開始湧出，只要順著發展，自然就能夠成就道德。這是所謂「善」的意義。而以惻隱之心為代表的這些道德開端，乃是人所獨有，且與禽獸有別的特殊之處。這特殊之處雖然看起來差別可能不大，但就這一點點的差異若能得以擴充，就會促成極大的差別。

　　《孟子》提出了人與禽獸不同之處，也提醒了我們人與禽獸也有相似之處。於是有人問，同樣是人，為什麼有些人的道德表現是君子，有些人則是小人？也就是說，既然所有人都普遍地具有上面說的那些道德起點，那為什麼不同的人道德表現會差那麼多？

　　凡是深刻的道德哲學家都必須回答這個問題。因為無論使用什麼樣的譬喻、用什麼樣的推論，從道德方面討論人性，原本都不外是為了回答「人為什麼會這樣？」「人應該做怎麼樣的事情？」「我們應該做什麼樣的人？」這些問題。

　　上文提到，人如果沒有那些道德起點就不算是個「人」，但人也絕非只有這些特性，我們也具有若干和動物類似的特性。在《孟子》裡，專屬於人而動物沒有的特性稱為「大體」；而除此之外和動物類似的特性，諸如感官、情緒、欲望等等本能則約略稱為「小體」。所有人都具有這兩面，重視「大體」這一面的人屬於有道德修養的人，反之則否；君子和小人的差別取決於個人選擇重視的面向。只要選擇重視自己天生的道德起點、並順著它的自然傾向發展，這就可以成就善。以上大致可說是《孟子》「性善說」的梗概。

　　至於「性惡說」則是出自《荀子》，原文字面大意是說人之性惡，如果有所謂善，那都是出自人為。這個說法大致是如此構成的：人天生都有感官知覺和欲望、情緒好惡等等，順著這些天生特性自然發展，難免會導致人際關係崩潰，社會秩序蕩然無存，所以需要人為的規範來加以導正節制。

　　為何這麼說呢？因為所有人天生都有些自然的欲望需要滿足，如果滿足欲望所需的資源不足以滿足所有人的需求，難免就會發生爭奪，如此人倫關係、社會秩序、甚至個人生存的安全都會受到威脅。所以文明傳統為我們各人賦予了社會角色和規範，讓我們追求欲望的行為有個分寸，如此方能避免爭奪與混亂。天生的欲望乃是自然生成，順著自然欲望而在人際關係當中發生爭奪與會亂，這就是所謂「惡」的意義；有了人為的規範，和諧與秩序所代表的「善」才可能出現。

　　如果人天生的欲望自然發展會導致上述所謂的「惡」，那麼人為的「善」是如何產生的？

　　所有深刻的道德哲學家也必須回答這個疑問。對此問題，《荀子》也提到了人除了具有會導致「惡」的天生性質，也具有一些有別於禽獸的特性。《荀子》所謂的天生之「性」不外是感官知覺、欲望、情緒之屬，其內容大致類似於《孟子》所說的「小體」；這些其實和禽獸的天性相去不遠。但上文清楚說到，順著這些天性發展會造成爭奪與混亂，因此需要人為的禮義規範來導正、節制。但這些人為的禮義規範是如何產生的？

　　如果只斷章取義地說禮義規範是來自上古的聖王，這只會將問題無限地延後、將我們迫切需要的答案推向無垠的遠處。因為，我們同樣可以問，古代的聖王既然也和我們一樣是人，那麼他們是如何制訂出促成和諧秩序的規範？

　　在此，《荀子》指出了人有別於禽獸的特性，只不過側重的面向和《孟子》有所不同。《孟子》說的是「惻隱之心」等天生的道德起點，《荀子》則說認為人天生有分辨是分的能力；憑著這種能力，人可以建立規範，依循此規範來建立人際關係、分配資源，因此我們可以優於禽獸。以上是性惡之說大致的脈絡。

選讀文本：

1.《孟子》論「性善」

(1) 孟子道性善，言必稱堯舜。〈滕文公上〉

(2) 孟子曰：「人皆有不忍人之心。先王有不忍人之心，斯有
不忍人之政矣。以不忍人之心，行不忍人之政，治天下可
運之掌上。所以謂人皆有不忍人之心者，今人乍見孺子將
入於井，皆有怵惕惻隱之心；非所以內交於孺子之父母也，
非所以要譽於鄉黨朋友也，非惡其聲而然也。由是觀之，
無惻隱之心非人也，無羞惡之心非人也，無辭讓之心非人
也，無是非之心非人也。惻隱之心，仁之端也；羞惡之心，
義之端也；辭讓之心，禮之端也；是非之心，智之端也。
人之有是四端也，猶其有四體也。有是四端而自謂不能者，
自賊者也；謂其君不能者，賊其君者也。凡有四端於我者，
知皆擴而充之矣，若火之始然、泉之始達。苟能充之，足
以保四海；苟不充之，不足以事父母。」〈公孫丑・上〉

(3) 孟子曰：「人之所以異於禽獸者幾希，庶民去之，君子存之。
舜明於庶物，察於人倫，由仁義行，非行仁義也。」〈離婁下〉

(4) 孟子曰：「乃若其情，則可以為善矣，乃所謂善也。若夫
為不善，非才之罪也。惻隱之心，人皆有之；羞惡之心，
人皆有之；恭敬之心，人皆有之；是非之心，人皆有之。
惻隱之心，仁也；羞惡之心，義也；恭敬之心，禮也；是
非之心，智也。仁義禮智，非由外鑠我也，我固有之也，

弗思耳矣。故曰：『求則得之，舍則失之。』或相倍蓰而無算者，不能盡其才者也。⋯⋯」〈告子・上〉

(5) 公都子問曰：「鈞是人也，或為大人，或為小人，何也？」孟子曰：「從其大體為大人，從其小體為小人。」曰：「鈞是人也，或從其大體，或從其小體，何也？」曰：「耳目之官不思，而蔽於物。物交物，則引之而已矣。心之官則思；思則得之，不思則不得也。此天之所與我者，先立乎其大者，則其小者不能奪也。此為大人而已矣。」〈告子上〉

2.《荀子》論「性惡」

(1) 人之性惡，其善者偽也。今人之性，生而有好利焉。順是，故爭奪生而辭讓亡焉。生而有疾惡焉。順是，故殘賊生而忠信亡焉。生而有耳目之欲，有好聲色焉。順是，故淫亂生而禮義亡焉。然則從人之性，順人之情，必出於爭奪，合於犯分亂理而歸於暴。故必將有師法之化、禮義之道，然後出於辭讓、合於文理而歸於治。用此觀之，然則人之性惡明矣，其善者偽也。〈性惡篇〉

(2) 禮起於何也？曰：人生而有欲，欲而不得，則不能無求。求而無度量分界，則不能不爭；爭則亂，亂則窮。先王惡其亂也，故制禮義以分之，以養人之欲，給人之求。使欲必不窮於物，物必不屈於欲。兩者相持而長，是禮之所起也。〈禮論篇〉

(3) 孟子曰：「人之性善。」曰：是不然。凡古今天下之所謂
善者，正理平治也；所謂惡者，偏險悖亂也：是善惡之分
也矣。〈性惡篇〉

(4) 凡性者、天之就也，不可學，不可事。禮義者、聖人之所
生也，人之所學而能，所事而成者也。不可學、不可事而
在人者，謂之性。可學而能、可事而成之在人者，謂之偽。
是性、偽之分也。

今人之性，飢而欲飽，寒而欲煖，勞而欲休，此人之情性也。
今人飢，見長不敢先食者，將有所讓也。勞而不敢求息者，
將有所代也。夫子之讓乎父，弟之讓乎兄；子之代乎父，
弟之代乎兄，此二行者，皆反於性而悖於情也。然而孝子
之道，禮義之文理也。故順情性則不辭讓矣，辭讓則悖於
情性矣。用此觀之，然則人之性惡明矣，其善者偽也。〈性
惡篇〉

(5) 人之所以為人者何已也？曰：以其有辨也。飢而欲食，寒
而欲煖，勞而欲息，好利而惡害，是人之所生而有也，是
無待而然者也，是禹、桀之所同也。然則人之所以為人者，
非特以二足而無毛也，以其有辨也。今夫狌狌形相亦二足
而無毛也，然而君子啜其羹，食其胾。故人之所以為人者，
非特以其二足而無毛也，以其有辨也。夫禽獸有父子而無
父子之親，有牝牡而無男女之別。故人道莫不有辨。〈非
相篇〉

問題討論：

1. 《孟子》說「惻隱之心，仁之端也」，請問這「端」字的意義與實際上成就道德的差別何在？

2. 《孟子》說「性善」的「善」意義為何？它和《荀子》所說「性惡」的「惡」是否針鋒相對？請從引文脈絡細細追索兩者各自的意義。

3. 《荀子》說「人之性惡」，這句話和「人性本惡」的差別何在？

4. 以上引文裡《孟子》所說的「性」字，和《荀子》所說的「性」字，兩者意義是否相同？如果相同，那麼，既然「性善」與「性惡」之說都是針對「人」而發，兩者說法是否沒有交集？如果兩說當中的「性」字意義不同，那麼，這兩種主張對於「人」之所以能成就道德的理由各自道出了什麼？

延伸閱讀：

1. 徐復觀，《中國人性論史》，臺北，臺灣學生書局，1987 年。

2. 朱熹，《四書章句集注》，北京，中華書局，2001 年。

3. 李滌生，《荀子集釋》，臺北，臺灣學生書局，1981 年。

十四、《孟子》、《韓非》論通權達變

王靈康

單元旨要：

　　當我們遇到一件事情需要下決定，或是需要評斷其是非對錯的時候，通常會參照前例，或是援用既有的原則。從前成功的例子，會在經驗的累積之下形成原則；而在時間中沉澱的原則，常指引著我們面對眼前的狀況，告訴我們如何抉擇、如何判斷。

　　這樣的方式通常有效；但世界隨時都充滿著變化，無論大自然的現象，或是人間的事態，都可能在下一刻出現前所未有的新狀況，有時候新狀況事關重大，考驗我們的能力、也挑戰著先人的智慧。如果遇上了前所未見的局面，而且又迫切需要解決，這時往昔成功的前例，和已經成為傳統的原則，就未必能夠為我們順利地解決問題，或者提供滿意的答覆。

　　這樣的情節在人類文明裡永遠反覆上演；今日如是，在上古亦如是。孟子身處的戰國時代中期，在政治和經濟上遭逢了前所未有的巨大變化，許多原本足以維持穩定生活的作法和原則都遇到了嚴峻的挑戰。孟子面對這種情勢，以譬喻的方式大膽提出了他的看法，認為在特殊且緊急的情況下，不但可以，而且應該放下成規，掌握當務之急的關鍵，採取隨機應變的作法。

　　在傳統社會生活的禮教之下，男女的分際本來絕對不可以踰越。與孟子對話的提問者即以此例構思了一個難題來挑戰：如果有個男子眼看著嫂嫂即將溺死，他可以伸出手來援救嗎？這在當時是違反男女授受不親之規範的。孟子明快地答道，嫂嫂溺水若不援救，這簡直是與豺狼無異。嚴守男女之防固然合乎禮教，但在性命攸關的時候以手相援，這叫通權達變。因為禮教固然在社會生活中有其必要，但相較之下，性命才是最根本的。提問者其實知道孟子會這麼回答，他目的是想激孟子採取比苦口婆心地講道理更強烈的手段來挽救時局。

　　接著孟子又遇上更敏感、更直接的挑戰。有人問孟子，據說夏朝的末代暴君是被當時居於臣下地位的商湯給放逐，而商朝的末代暴君也是被當時居於下位的武王給討伐的，有這麼回事嗎？孟子答道，歷史上是這麼記載的。提問者直接地問道：「臣下弒君上，這樣可以嗎？」這個問題是想將孟子逼進兩難。孟子若說臣下可以弒君，則這是違背禮法；若孟子按著禮法說臣下絕不可以弒君，那就是承認了暴君的正當性。此處既質疑了孟子秉持的禮法傳統，也挑戰了孟子講仁義的道德核心。君臣之義固然是維繫秩序的綱紀，但在道德的核心價值之下，無論不仁之君或不義之臣，都已經失去各自的名分原本具有的內涵。因此，歷史上的湯與武王各自對當時暴君所採取的行動，雖然不合乎形式上名分所應遵守的規範，但在深一層的義蘊之下，卻更合乎道德的價值。所以孟子的作法是用道德的價值重新衡量統治者的正當性，以此化解了法統與道德的兩難。

　　看過從前市場上用的桿秤嗎？一根有刻度的桿子上，一端掛著要秤的東西，另一端有個可以移動的秤錘，兩端之間的提環可以將整個秤提起。秤東西的時候，藉著移動秤錘來取得平衡。東西若是重，就將秤錘離中

間的提環遠些；若是輕，就把秤錘靠提環近些。兩端平衡的時候，根據秤錘所在之處的刻度就知道重量了。孟子說的「權」就好比秤錘。我們就是靠著可以移動的秤錘才能在變動中取得平衡。傳統的規範是固定的、不宜輕易變動的；但若是遇上極為特殊的情況就必須有所權衡了。例如，男女授受不親固須謹守，但面對性命攸關的情況，若由維護生命這更高的價值著眼，當然要有不同的具體作法。

孟子非常講究審視具體情況而採取適當的權變，但是又不能失去核心價值。這當然需要高度的智慧，若非經過陶養難以達到。因此，在尚未達這種境界之前，我們不免設想，如果能在兩個極端之間找個折衷之處，是否就算是得宜的權衡？然而孟子卻提醒，在兩個極端間取其折衷，固然避免了極端，但若因此就將這種折衷視為理所當然，則又失去了權變的意義，因為這和墨守其中任何一端是一樣的，都是死守而不知變通，這反而會傷害了「道」。當時的楊子主張「為我」，拔一毛而利天下都不肯，墨子摩頂放踵，樂於為天下人奉獻犧牲。但在孟子看來，楊子顯然不及，墨子顯然超過，這兩者都不符合中道精神，都不足以作為天下人行為的準則。對於父母子女與路人，本有親疏遠近的關係，人當依此關係決定自己的行為，如果一視同仁，不論只顧自己、或者不分親疏兼愛天下、或者在這裡兩者之間找個簡單的折衷作法，都不算是妥善地解決問題。

韓非是戰國時代最晚期的思想家之一，他綜觀古史，認為歷代名君聖主的功業之所以為後世所景仰，是因為他們的所作所為切合當時的需求。他將過往的歷史分為上古、中古和近古：上古的領袖解決了人民基本生存需求的問題，中古的君王解決了水患，近古的君王以征伐解決了外患。至於他所身處的時代，面臨的是截然不同的動亂。如果當今的在位者仍然

不能看清楚時代的需求，而企圖仿效往昔統治者成功的作為，就是昧於現實。不同的時代有不同的問題，不同的問題需要不同的對策。如果只能緬懷昔日的盛世，還想以從前的方式來治理天下，就好比那農夫只因曾經憑著偶然的運氣抓到兔子，就放下了該作的事情，終日期待好運再度降臨，完全不能認清自己當下面臨的問題是什麼，更別說拿出有效的辦法來解決。

　　戰國時代是古代中國歷史變動最劇烈的第一個階段，各家的哲人依循著各自繼承的傳統智慧提出對策，但也反思到往昔曾經有效的原則或方法未必能夠面對日新月異的變局，因此語重心長地提醒我們要能夠審時度勢，通權達變。

選讀文本：

1.《孟子》

(1)

淳于髡曰：「男女授受不親，禮與？」

孟子曰：「禮也。」

曰：「嫂溺則援之以手乎？」

曰：「嫂溺不援，是豺狼也。男女授受不親，禮也；嫂溺援之以手者，權也。」

《孟子・離婁上》

(2)

齊宣王問曰：「湯放桀，武王伐紂，有諸？」

孟子對曰：「於傳有之。」

曰：「臣弒其君，可乎？」

曰：「賊仁者，謂之賊；賊義者，謂之殘。殘賊之人，謂之一夫。聞誅一夫紂矣，未聞弒君也。」《孟子・梁惠王下》

(3)

　　孟子曰：「楊子取為我，拔一毛而利天下，不為也。墨子兼愛，摩頂放踵利天下，為之。子莫執中，執中為近之，執中無權，猶執一也。所惡執一者，為其賊道也，舉一而廢百也。」《孟子·盡心上》

2.《韓非子》

　　上古之世，人民少而禽獸眾，人民不勝禽獸蟲蛇，有聖人作，構木為巢以避群害，而民悅之，使王天下，號曰有巢氏。民食果蓏蚌蛤，腥臊惡臭而傷害腹胃，民多疾病，有聖人作，鑽燧取火以化腥臊，而民說之，使王天下，號之曰燧人氏。

　　中古之世，天下大水，而鯀、禹決瀆。近古之世，桀、紂暴亂，而湯、武征伐。今有構木鑽燧於夏后氏之世者，必為鯀、禹笑矣。有決瀆於殷、周之世者，必為湯、武笑矣。

　　然則今有美堯、舜、湯、武、禹之道於當今之世者，必為新聖笑矣。是以聖人不期脩古，不法常可，論世之事，因為之備。宋人有耕田者，田中有株，兔走，觸株折頸而死，因釋其耒而守株，冀復得兔，兔不可復得，而身為宋國笑。今欲以先王之政，治當世之民，皆守株之類也。《韓非子·五蠹》

問題討論：

1.「聞誅一夫紂矣，未聞弒君也」這樣的想法，可以說具有現代的民主思想嗎？為什麼？

2.「執中無權，猶執一也」的意義是什麼？《孟子》為什麼不同意？您能否在日常生活中舉出幾個例子來說明？

3.《韓非子》所說的「守株待兔」可笑、可議之處究竟何在？您可以就日常生活舉出些例子嗎？

延伸閱讀：

1.《四書章句集注》，北京，中華書局，1983 年。

2.《韓非子集解》，北京，中華書局，1998 年。

十五、《荀子》論自然之天

王靈康

單元旨要：

自遠古以來，人類對於大自然始終充滿好奇、又帶著幾分畏懼，然而卻又對它有所期待。它浩瀚無垠，深不可測，也變化無常。當它帶來滋養生命的資源，我們享用之餘會對不知何以名之的對象心存感激，也期待來年再度賜予豐收。當它帶來無可抗拒的災厄，我們除了怨嘆、掙扎、懼怕，還希望自己能做些什麼來祈求它憐憫悅納。

於是，它變成了祂。

祂的樣貌不可見不可聞；祂的心意無從揣測，祂的能力無可匹敵，祂的行止迎之不見其首，隨之不見其後。人們視它為生命的來源和主宰、所有生成變化之現象的原因和目的、一切價值標準的依歸，包括道德行為的準則。對各種形式之神明的信仰，是不同文明的象徵，也是各民族生活方式的依據。常常，我們以祂最可見的形式（「天」）一來稱呼祂。然而，隨著文明的發展，人類累積了與大自然奮鬥的經驗，漸漸發現，原來「天」未必那麼神祕，未必那麼可怕。只要長久細心大量地觀察自然現象的變化，或多或少能摸索到一些變化的規律；只要能預先推測自然的變化，就能準備未來將發生的是滋養還是災難；常常見到好人沒好報，惡人沒惡報，也許會懷疑上天真的是賞善罰惡的正義主宰嗎？

於是，對某些人來說，祂變回了它。

在西方宗教文明發展的途中，曾經出現過解除上天之魔咒的思想，人們企圖用自己的理智來看待自然，用自己的智慧來決定命運。雖然神明並未就此遜位，但是這方興未艾的思潮也影響了人看待自然、看待天、看待自己的方式。

在中國古代將「天」奉為價值主宰的信仰傳統之下，也曾有過將「天」純然視為「自然現象」的思想曇花一現。《荀子》裡的〈天論〉針對戰國時期的天命思想傳統發言，認為社稷的運勢並非取決於上天是否認可統治者的行為，而端視統治者是否能有智慧地應對自然現象的運行。

如果上天對人世傳達訊息，常常是透過不尋常的自然現象，有人是這麼相信的。但，如果認為人間的道德與自然現象無關、也不認為上天會干預人間的事，當不尋常的自然現象出現的時候，他並不會感到驚恐，因為他不認為超自然的力量會藉此介入人世，無須為此驚恐。這些現象都只是天地之間較罕見自然的變化；好奇可以，害怕就不對了。

天地間的自然變化，經過長期的觀察，可以呈現出某種規律，這些規律並不會因為統治者的道德表現而有所不同。無論大自然帶給我們什麼樣的情況，只要用合理的方式面對它就是好事，用不合理的方式面對它就是壞事。好與壞取決於我們如何應對，這些現象本身只是自然地來到了我們的世界，並不是針對人的道德而發的訊息。

偶然發生不尋常的現象，這是任何時代都會有的事情。如果在君主賢明、政治穩定的時期，發生這些事情也不會有什麼害處；如果君主昏庸、

政治混亂，即便任何自然異象都有沒發生，也不表示有任何好處。

　　這樣的想法有何基礎？就是因為相信天地的變化是依循它自然的道理，不是因為有個主宰對人間統治者的作為有所感應，因而降下福祉或災禍。在人間就作人間該做的事，用人間的道理人處理人間的問題。加強生產，就不怕饑荒；節約開支，就不虞匱乏。人們的生活資源充足、適當運動，就不用擔心生病。循著合理的原則處理事情，就不怕天降災難。所以旱災水災都不會讓人餓、天冷天熱也無法讓人病，什麼怪事也都不會帶來災難。

　　但若荒廢了生產，忘記了基本該做的事情，而且又不能控制支出，這樣上天也沒辦法讓我們富足。人們基本生活之所需不足，又不講求適時運動，那麼上天也無法賜我們健康。為政處事背離了合理的原則，那麼上天也無法帶來好運。如果是這樣，即便沒有旱災水災，也難保不發生饑荒；人即便沒有寒暑侵身，也難保不會生病；就算不發生什麼怪事，厄運也難免到來。

　　災難來到的時候，我們自問，明明處在和治世同樣的天時，為什麼這些會降臨在我們身上？這難道可以怨天？如果天只是自然地運轉，那麼亂世和治世的差別，是否只在於處理人世間的事情應該照合乎人世之道理的作法，而不需祈求上天的垂憐？

選讀文本：

1.

星隊，木鳴，國人皆恐。

曰：是何也？曰：無何也！是天地之變，陰陽之化，物之罕至者也。怪之可也；而畏之非也。夫日月之有蝕，風雨之不時，怪星之黨見，是無世而不常有之。上明而政平，則是雖並世起，無傷也；上闇而政險，則是雖無一至者，無益也。

2.

天行有常，不為堯存，不為桀亡。

應之以治則吉，應之以亂則凶。

彊本而節用，則天不能貧；

養備而動時，則天不能病；

脩道而不貳，則天不能禍。

故水旱不能使之饑，寒暑不能使之疾，祅怪不能使之凶。

本荒而用侈，則天不能使之富；

養略而動罕，則天不能使之全；

倍道而妄行，則天不能使之吉。

故水旱未至而饑，寒暑未薄而疾，祅怪未至而凶。

受時與治世同，而殃禍與治世異，不可以怨天，其道然也。

故明於天人之分，則可謂至人矣。

……

治亂天邪？曰：日月、星辰、瑞曆，是禹、桀之所同也，禹以治，桀以亂，治亂非天也。時邪？曰：繁啟蕃長於春夏，畜積收藏於秋冬，是又禹、桀之所同也，禹以治，桀以亂，治亂非時也。地邪？曰：得地則生，失地則死，是又禹桀之所同也，禹以治，桀以亂，治亂非地也。

《荀子‧天論》

問題討論：

1. 這樣的想法和歷史上的「君權神授」差異何在？

2. 本單元的引文若放在現代，可以給我們什麼樣的啟示？

3. 科學昌明的今日，對於超自然的信仰卻從未消失，請問這是為什麼？
   信仰和迷信有何不同？

延伸閱讀：

1. 李滌生，《荀子集釋》，臺北，臺灣學生書局，2000 年。

2. 韋政通，《荀子與古代哲學》，臺北，臺灣商務印書館，1992 年。

十六、《菩提達磨》閱讀

張 國 一

單元旨要：

　　達磨（？-530)，在中國，是一位家喻戶曉的佛門人物。許多與他相關聯的神祕故事，如：面壁九年、一葦渡江、隻履西歸，乃至說他創造了易筋經、一掌金等武俠、占卜之術，都廣大流傳起來。不過，這大多是缺乏根據，不值得信賴的編造、創作。

　　達磨為西域南天竺人，大約在南朝劉宋 (420-470) 年間，經海路，抵達了中國。他宣揚眾生即佛、人人皆具備圓滿佛性的印度「如來藏學」，特重弘闡《楞伽經》，成為中國禪宗的初祖。不過，他在世時，禪門，尚未見重於中國佛教，還要經過大略一百年，他播下的這顆種子，才在中國大放異彩，興盛起來。

　　今天，我們想要理解、探究達磨，應參考哪些較可信賴的資料？最重要的一篇材料，即本文所選取的《菩提達磨大師略辨大乘入道四行及序》。

　　《菩提達磨大師略辨大乘入道四行及序》，達磨弟子曇琳 (約 585 年卒) 所記寫。文分為兩部分，首先為《序》，為若干關於達磨生平的記錄。北魏楊衒之的《洛陽伽藍記》(約作於 547 年)，亦較早記錄有達磨

生平的文獻，然僅寥寥數語而已。探究達磨生平，曇琳《序》，為目前，最重要、值得參考的一篇文字。[1]

其次，曇琳在《序》後，收錄了達磨傳授「入道」的禪法──「二入四行」。

「二入」，乃為「理入」、「行入」。

「理入」，就是要能「深信含生，同一真性，但為客塵妄想所覆，不能顯了。」也就是深信：眾生皆佛，人人皆具足佛性，應先有此一自我肯定。

而後，才可進入修行──「行入」，也就是「四行」。包括了：1. 逢苦不憂，知是業報現行的「報冤行」；2. 識一切緣生緣滅，無可執著的「隨緣行」；3. 知萬法皆空，故無貪求的「無所求行」；4. 修行六度，自利利他，實無所行的「稱法行」。

「二入四行」，乃站在人人具足佛性，但為煩惱遮蔽，故不得見之的「如來藏學」立場，從簡易、人人可從的俗諦──「報冤行」出發，逐漸「隨緣」入空，進入深徹、勝義的「無所求行」中，再轉小為大，修六度，利眾生，行而無行，最終證入「稱法行」之圓滿位階。

這確實是一套極為簡要、深徹、完備，引人「入道」的禪修指南！修「二入四行」，自然，遂契入大乘佛教之圓滿內涵：般若（證空）、慈悲（度眾而

---

[1] 以上關於達磨之生平、著作，主要參考了印順：《中國禪宗史》第一章：「菩提達磨之禪」。

實無所行）的法性、性海中了。

這一篇「二入四行」禪要，大略，也是我們目前，探究達磨思想，最重要，甚至是唯一一種，值得參考、信賴的材料。

透過閱讀、理解《菩提達磨大師略辨大乘入道四行及序》，達磨，這位中國歷史上，知名廣大、神祕、謎樣的人物，大略，我們可稍微恢復其幾分「本來面目」了。

《菩提達磨大師略辨大乘入道四行及序》，目前，被收錄在《卍續藏經》110 冊，807-808 頁中。文末，附有南朝梁武帝蕭衍之〈達磨大師碑頌〉，本文亦一併展示之，可備一考。

選讀文本：

1.曇琳序

　　法師者，西域南天竺國人，是婆羅門國王第三之子也。神慧疎朗，聞皆曉悟，志存摩訶衍道。故捨素隨緇，紹隆聖種，冥心虛寂，通鑒世事，內外俱明，德超世表。

　　悲悔邊隅，正教陵替，遂能遠涉山海，遊化漢魏。亡心之士，莫不歸信；存見之流，乃生譏謗。

　　于時唯有道育、惠可，此二沙門，年雖後生，俊志高遠。幸逢法師，事之數載，虔恭諮[2]啟，善蒙師意。法師感其精誠，誨以真道，令如是安心，如是發行，如是順物，如是方便。

　　此是大乘安心之法，令無錯謬。如是安心者，壁觀；如是發行者，四行；如是順物者，防護譏嫌；如是方便者，遣其不著。此略序所由云爾。

2.正文

　　夫入道多途，要而言之，不出二種：一是理入，二是行入。

　　理入者，謂藉教悟宗。深信含生，同一真性，但為客塵妄想所覆，不

---

[2] 原脫此一「諮」字，據《卍續藏經》校正之。

能顯了。若也捨妄歸真，凝住壁觀，無自無他，凡聖等一，堅住不移，更不隨文教。此即與理冥符，無有分別，寂然無為，名之理入。

行入，謂四行，其餘諸行，悉入此中。何等四耶？一、報冤行，二、隨緣行，三、無所求行，四、稱法行。

一、云何報冤行？謂修道行人，若受苦時，當自念言：我往昔無數劫中，棄本從末，流浪諸有，多起冤憎，違害無限，今雖無犯，是我宿殃，惡業果熟，非天非人，所能見與，甘心甘受，都無冤訴。經云：逢苦不憂。何以故？識達故。此心生時，與理相應，體冤進道，故說言報冤行。

二、隨緣行者，眾生無我，並緣業所轉，苦樂齊受，皆從緣生。若得勝報榮譽等事，是我過去宿因所感，今方得之，緣盡還無，何喜之有？得失從緣，心無增減，喜風不動，冥順於道，是故說言隨緣行。

三、無所求行者，世人長迷，處處貪著，名之為求。智者悟真，理將俗反，安心無為，形隨運轉，萬有斯空，無所願樂。功德黑暗，常相隨逐，三界久居，猶如火宅，有身皆苦，誰得而安？了達此處，故捨諸有，止想無求。經曰：有求皆苦，無求即樂。判知無求，真為道行，故言無所求行。

四、稱法行者，性淨之理，目之為法。此理眾相斯空，無染無著，無此無彼。經曰：法無眾生，離眾生垢故；法無有我，離我垢故。智者若能信解此理，應當稱法而行。法體無慳，身命財，行檀捨施，心無悋惜。脫解三空，不倚不著，但為去垢，稱化眾生，而不取相。此為自行，復能利他，亦能莊嚴菩提之道。檀施既爾，餘五亦然，為除妄想，修行六度，而無所行，是為稱法行。

3. 梁武帝蕭衍〈達磨大師碑頌〉

楞伽山頂坐寶日，中有金人披縷褐，

形同大地體如空，心如瑠璃色如雪。

匪磨匪瑩恒淨明，披雲卷霧心且微，

芬陀利花用嚴身，隨緣䚰物常怡[3]悅。

不有不無非去來，多聞辨才無法說，

實哉空哉離生有，大之小之眾緣絕。

刹那而登妙覺心，躍鱗慧海起先哲，

理應法水永長流，何期暫涌還蹔渴。

驪龍珠內落心燈，白毫慧刃當鋒欼，

生途忽焉[4]慧眼閉，禪河駐流法梁折。

無去無來無是非，彼此形體心碎裂，

住焉去焉[5]皆歸寂，寂內何曾存哽咽。

用之執手以傳燈，生死去來如電掣，

有能至誠心不疑，劫火燃燈斯不滅，

一真之法盡可有，未悟迷途茲是渴。

---

[3] 原「次」字，據《卍續藏經》校正為「怡」

[4] 原「鳥」字，據《卍續藏經》校正為「焉」。

[5] 原「住鳥去鳥」，據《卍續藏經》校正為「住焉去焉」。

問題討論：

1. 請問我們目前想要研究達磨生平、思想，有哪些文獻，是值得信賴，可以參考的？

2. 請問印度「如來藏學」思想，其義涵為何？

3. 根據《菩提達磨大師略辨大乘入道四行及序》一文，請嘗試理解、分析，禪悟的內涵，究竟為何？

4. 達磨有「二入四行」文記傳世，並且，看重弘闡《楞伽經》，這和我們一般對禪宗「不立文字」的理解，有些不同。請問禪宗，關於經典、文字，他們的態度，究竟為何？

延伸閱讀：

1. 楊衒之，《洛陽伽藍記》，臺北，三民書局，2006 年。

2. 釋印順，《中國禪宗史》，臺北，正聞出版社，1992 年。

3. 釋悟顯講述，《達磨二入四行觀》，臺北，大乘定香精舍，2013 年。

4. 釋果如，《達磨與你同行：覓一個不受惑的人》，新北市，大千出版社，2013 年。

5. 蔡志忠，《漫畫達磨禪》，臺北，大塊文化出版，2013 年。

十七、《六祖壇經》選讀

張國一

單元旨要：

禪宗，開啟於南北朝之菩提達磨，經慧可、僧燦、道信、弘忍等禪者100多年的承繼、宏揚，進入唐代，在惠能 (638-713) 手中，終發展成廣傳、普及、「凡言禪者皆歸曹溪」的燦爛新階段。

惠能，為中國禪史中，一承先開後，改革創新，揚宗興教的偉大宗匠！

一種一般的流行說法是，禪，原為漸悟、漸修的，在惠能手中，被改革成為頓悟、頓修！此一新禪法，在中國，迅速得到了廣大重視、認同、歡迎，竟打敗了其他中國佛教諸宗：天台、華嚴、唯識等，以一支獨秀之姿，成為中國佛教之正宗、代表者，屹立不搖，迄於今日！

此一說法，大略不錯吧！不過，惠能自己不是也說：「法無頓漸，人有利鈍，迷即漸勸，悟人頓修。」(詳下文)「漸勸」、「頓修」，為因材施教兩種不同方法，惠能禪，對他們實在是兼容並包的。

惠能對傳統禪法最大的改造，大略是特別對於「禪悟」的看重！

修道，無論為禪門，或其他宗派，本以明心見性、悟道解脫為目標、

目的。然大多數人，竟忘記了此一修道本懷，追逐於禪定、義學、經教、神通這些枝微末節去了。

惠能大聲疾呼，修道，只是為了和佛祖一般，得到一顆平靜、智慧、解脫、自由的心，也就是「禪悟」，這是修道唯一的目的，其餘都只是過程、次要的、衍伸的。一個旅行者，不當耽戀旅途景觀，應確立其目的地，念茲在茲，方可能真正完成旅程！

從這個觀點來看，惠能並不是一個動機論者，他更強調目標、目的的達成！

此無異為一當頭棒喝！把所有的佛教修道者，都敲醒了！禪門，也就從此確立了其明確的、徹底的、究竟的、無可匹敵的宗教方向—唯求明心見性、悟道成佛，此外，一法不立！

忽而，整個中國佛教界，竟皆認同之，紛紛投身、參與進入此一洪流中了！

惠能的大聲疾呼，最重要、最完整的一次，應屬在「韶州大梵寺」的演講、傳法。弟子法海等人，把它記錄了下來，也就是本文所呈現的這部《南宗頓教最上大乘摩訶般若波羅蜜經六祖惠能大師於韶州大梵寺施法壇經》。

《壇經》在歷史的流傳上，被經過多次的改造，主要分成兩個系統：惠昕本《壇經》（約 14,000 字）、契嵩本《壇經》（約 20,000 字）。本文所呈現者，為最古，較接近原始風貌，較可信賴的敦煌本《壇經》（約共

12,000 字）。它在 1923 年，被矢吹慶輝先生發現，並於 1928 年，被編入《大正藏》第 48 卷。這是我們目前探究惠能生平、思想，最重要、值得信賴的資料。

不過，敦煌本《壇經》，是一個劣本，錯字很多，本文在校寫上，主要又參考了楊增文新校敦博本《壇經》的研究成果。

並且，限於篇幅，只能節選敦煌本《壇經》中，較重要的文字。關於大梵寺開法的主軸：「說摩訶般若波羅蜜」，整段文字都收錄了。惠能最重要的禪學思想，廣說「定慧一體」、「一行三昧」、「無念為宗、無相為體、無住為本」、「坐禪」、「禪定」的演講，我們也收錄了。開法結束，學人提問，本文挑選了「梁武帝有無功德」、「西方極樂世界」兩段問答。

雖僅為節選，然關於惠能最重要的禪學思想，大抵於此已可窺見一般！

惠能禪，揭示、確立了中國佛教發展的新方向，以海納百川之姿，領頭向前！修道，目標、目的，必須先正確確立，這樣，便不會走遠路，也不會走錯路！一心一志在此，頓修也好，漸修也好，讀經也好，不讀經也好，終要走上開悟見性，成佛做祖，解脫自由的大道上。

一般以為禪門，是輕視經典、不立文字的。其實，那出於一種嚴重的誤解。惠能本人，就是《金剛般若波羅蜜經》的宏揚、提倡者（詳下）。方法，為其次，確立目標，才是最重要的。目標確立了，該如何去達成？因材施教，可有千變萬化，靈活巧妙的多般施設了！

惠能開啟之「禪」，從此，竟成為中國佛教的代名詞！

閱讀文本[1]：

1. 廣說定慧一體、一行三昧、坐禪等

　　惠能大師喚言：善知識，菩提般若之智[2]，世人本自有之，即緣心迷，不能自悟，須求大善知識示道見性。善知識，遇悟成智。善知識，我此法門，以定慧[3]為本，第一勿迷言慧定別。定慧體一不二，即定是慧體，即慧是定用。即慧之時定在慧，即定之時慧在定。善知識，此義即是定[4]慧等。學道之人作意，莫言先定發慧，先慧發定，定慧各別。作此見者，法有二相，口說善，心不善，慧定不等。心口俱善，內外一種[5]，定慧即等。自悟修行，不在口諍，若諍先後，即是迷[6]人，不斷勝負，却生法我，不離四相。

　　一行三昧者，於一切時中，行住坐[7]臥常真，直心[8]是。《淨名經》云：「直心是道場，直心是淨土。」莫心行諂曲，口說法直，口說一行三昧，不行直心，非佛弟子。但行直心，於一切法上無有執著，名一行三昧。迷人著法相，執一行三昧，直心坐不動，除妄不起心，即是一行三昧，

---

[1] 以下文字，底本為敦煌本，若有可疑字、錯字，皆根據楊曾文校訂敦博新本進行改定。

[2] 原作「知」。

[3] 原作「定惠」改成「定慧」，以下皆同。

[4] 原缺「定」字。

[5] 原作「一眾種」。

[6] 原缺「迷」字。

[7] 原作「座」，改成「坐」，以下皆同。。

[8] 原作「真心」，改成「直心」，以下皆同。。

若如是，此法同無情[9]，却是障道因緣。道順通流，何以却滯？心不住法，道即通流，[10]住即被[11]縛，若坐不動，是維摩詰不合呵舍利弗宴坐林中。

善知識，又見有人教人坐，看心看淨，不動不起，從此置功，迷人不悟，便執成顛。即有數百般[12]，如此教道者，故知[13]大錯。善知識，定慧猶如何等？如燈光，有燈即有光，無燈即無光，燈是光之[14]體，光是燈之用，名[15]即有二，體無兩般，此定慧法，亦復如是。善知識，法無頓漸，人有利鈍，迷[16]即漸勸，悟人頓修。識自本是見本性，悟即元無差別，不悟即長劫輪迴。

善知識，我此法門，從上已來，頓漸皆立無念為宗、無相為體、無住為本。何名[17]為相無相？於相而離相。無念者，於念而不念。無住者，為人本性，念念不住，前念、今[18]念、後念，念念相續，無有斷絕，若一念斷絕，法身即是離色身。念念時中，於一切法上無住，一念若住，念念即住，名繫縛。於一切法上，念念不住，即無縛也，以無住為本。

---

[9] 原作「清」。

[10] 原作「心住在即通流」。

[11] 原作「彼」。

[12] 原作「盤」。

[13] 原作「之」。

[14] 原作「知」。

[15] 原缺「名」字。

[16] 原作「明」。

[17] 原作「明」。

[18] 原作「念」。

　　善知識，外離一切相，是無相，但能離相，性體清淨[19]，是以無相為體。於一切境上不染，名為無念，於自念上離境，不於法上念生。莫百物不思，念盡除却，一念斷即死，別處受生。學道者用心，莫不識[20]法意，自錯尚可，更勸他人，迷不自見迷，又謗經法。是以立無念為宗，即緣迷人於境上有念，念上便起邪見，一切塵勞妄念，從此而生。

　　然此教門，立無念為宗，世人離見，不起於念，若無有念，無念亦不立。無者無何事？念者何物？無者，離二相諸塵勞，真如是念之體，念是真如之用。自[21]性起念，雖即見聞覺知，不染萬境而常自在。《維摩經》云：「外能善分別諸法相，內於第一義而不動。」

　　善知識，此法門中，坐禪元不著心，亦不著淨，亦不言動。若言看心，心元是妄，妄如幻故，無所看也。若言看淨，人性本淨，為妄念故，蓋覆真如，離妄念，本性淨。不見自性本淨，心起看淨，却生淨妄，妄無處所，故知看[22]却是妄也。淨無形相，却立淨相，言是功夫，作此見者，障[23]自本性，却被淨縛。若不動者，不[24]見一切人過患，是性不動，迷人自身不動，開口即說人是非，與道違背。看心、看淨，却是障道因緣。

　　今既如是[25]，此法門中，何名坐禪？此法門中，一切無礙，外於一切

---

[19] 原作「性體清淨是」。

[20] 原作「息」。

[21] 原缺「自」字。

[22] 原作「看者看」。

[23] 原作「章」。

[24] 「不」字為筆者所增入者。

[25] 原作「今記汝是」。

境界上，念不去為坐，見本性不亂為禪。何名為禪定？外離[26]相曰禪，內不亂曰定，外若有相，內心即亂，外若離相，[27]內性不亂。本自淨自定，只緣境觸，觸即亂。離相不亂即定，外離相即禪，內[28]不亂即定，外禪內定，故名禪定。《維摩經》云：「即時[29]豁然，還得本心。」《菩薩戒經[30]》云：「戒本源自性清淨。[31]」善知識，見自性自淨，自修自作，自性法身，自行佛行，自作自成佛道。

2. 正說摩訶般若波羅蜜

摩訶般若波羅蜜者，西國梵語，唐言大智慧到彼岸[32]。此法須行，不在口念[33]，口念不行，如幻[34]如化，修行者，法身與佛等也。

何名摩訶？摩訶者是大。心量廣大，猶如虛空，莫空[35]心坐，即落無記[36]空，世界虛空，[37]能含日月星辰、大地山河、一切草木、惡人善人、

---

[26] 原作「雜」。

[27] 原缺「內心即亂，外若離相」八字。

[28] 原作「內外」。

[29] 原作「是」。

[30] 原缺「經」字。

[31] 原作「本須自性清淨」。

[32] 原作「彼岸到」。

[33] 原缺「念」字。

[34] 原缺「幻」字。

[35] 原作「定」。

[36] 原作「既」。

[37] 原無「世界虛空」四字。

惡法善法、天堂地獄，盡在空中，世人性空，亦復如是。性含萬法是大，萬法盡是自性，見一切人及非人、惡之[38]與善、惡法善法，盡皆不捨，不可染著，猶[39]如虛空，名之為大。此是摩訶行，迷人口念，智者心行[40]。又有迷[41]人，空心不思，名之為大，此亦不是。心量大，不行是少，莫口空說，不修此行，非我弟子。

何名般若？般若是智慧。一切[42]時中，念念不愚，常行智慧，即名般若。行一念愚，即般若絕，一念智，即般若生。世人心中常愚，自言我修般若，[43]般若無形相，智慧性即是。

何名波羅蜜？此是西國梵音，言到彼岸[44]，解義離生滅。著境[45]生滅起[46]，如水有波浪，即是於此岸；離境無生滅，如水承長流，故即名到彼岸，故名波羅蜜。迷人口念，智者心行。當念時有妄，有妄即非真有，念念若行，是名真有。悟此法者，悟般若法，修般若行，不修即凡，一念修行，法身等佛。善知識，即煩惱是菩提，前[47]念迷即凡，後念悟即佛。

善知識，摩訶般若波羅蜜，最尊最上第一，無住無去無來，三世諸

---

[38] 原作「知」。

[39] 原作「由」。

[40] 原缺「行」字。

[41] 原作「名」。

[42] 原缺「切」字。

[43] 原作「心中常愚，我修」六字。

[44] 原作「彼岸到」。

[45] 原作「竟」。

[46] 原作「去」。

[47] 原作「捉前」。

佛從中出。將大知慧到彼岸，打破五陰煩惱塵勞，最尊最上第一，讚最上乘法，[48] 修行定成佛。無去無住無來往，是定慧等，不染一切法，三世諸佛從中出[49]，變三毒為戒定慧。善知識，我此法門，從一般若生八萬四千智慧，[50] 何以故？為世有八萬四千塵勞，若無塵勞，般若常在，不離自性。

悟此法者，即是無念、無憶[51]、無著，莫起雜妄[52]，即自是真如性用，智慧[53] 觀照，於一切法不取不捨，即見性成佛道。善知識，若欲入甚深法界，入般若三昧者，直修般若波羅蜜行。但持《金剛般若波羅蜜經》一卷，即得見性，入般若三昧，當知此人功德無量，經中分明[54] 讚嘆，不能具說。

3. 梁武帝有無功德、西方極樂世界之問答

大師說法了，韋使君、官僚[55]、僧眾、道俗，讚言無盡，昔所未聞。使君禮拜自言：「和尚說法，實不思議，弟子當有少疑，欲問[56] 和尚，望意和尚大慈大悲，為弟子說」。大師言：「有疑即問，[57] 何須再三。」

---

[48] 原作「讚最上最上乘法」。

[49] 原缺「出」字。

[50] 原作「從八萬四千智慧」。

[51] 原作「億」。

[52] 原作「莫去誰妄」。

[53] 原作「知惠」。

[54] 原作「名」。

[55] 原作「寮」。

[56] 原作「聞」。

[57] 原作「有議即聞」。

　　使君問[58]：「法可不是[59]西國第一祖達磨祖師宗旨？」。大師言：「是。」「弟子見說，達磨大師化[60]梁武帝[61]，帝[62]問達磨：『朕一生以[63]來，造寺、布施、供養，有[64]功德否？』達磨答言：『並無功德』。武帝惆悵，遂遣達磨出境。未審此言，請和尚說。」

　　六祖言：「實無功德，使君勿疑[65]，達磨大師言武帝著邪道，不識正法。」使君問：「何以無功德？」和尚言：「造寺、布施、供養，只是修福，不可將福以為功德。功德[66]在法身，非在於福田，自法性有功德，平直是德，佛性外行恭敬，若輕一切人，吾[67]我不斷，即自無功德。自性虛妄，法身無功德，念念行[68]平等真心，德即不輕，常行於敬。自修身即功，自修身心即德，功德自心作，福與功德別，武帝不識正理，非祖大師有過。」

　　使君禮拜，又問：「弟子見僧道俗，常念阿彌陀[69]佛，願往生西方，請和尚說，得[70]生彼否？望為破疑。」大師言：「使君聽，惠能與說。世

[58] 原作「聞」。

[59] 原作「不不是」。

[60] 原作「代」。

[61] 原缺「帝」字。

[62] 原作「諦」。

[63] 原作「未」。

[64] 原作「有有」。

[65] 原作「朕勿疑」。

[66] 原缺「功德」二字。

[67] 原作「悟」。

[68] 原作「德行」。

[69] 原作「大」。

[70] 原作「德」。

尊在舍衛國，說西方引化，經文分明，去此不遠，只為下根說遠，說近只緣上智。[71]人自兩重，法無兩般[72]，悟有殊，見有遲疾。迷人念佛生彼，悟者自淨其心，所以佛言[73]，隨其心淨，則佛土淨。」

「使君，東方人[74]但淨心無罪，西方人[75]心不淨有愆。迷人願生東方，兩[76]者所在處，並皆一種。心但無不淨，西方去此不遠，心起不淨之心，念佛往生難到。除十[77]惡即行十萬，無八邪即過八千，但行真心，到如禪指。使君，但行十善，何須更願往生？不斷十惡之心，何佛即來迎請？若悟無生頓法，見西方只在剎那，不悟頓教大乘，念佛往生路遙，如何得達？」

六祖言：「惠能與使君移西方剎那間[78]，目[79]前便見，使君願見否？」使君禮拜：「若此得見，何須往生？願和尚慈悲，為現西方，大善！」大師言：「唐見西方，無疑即散。」大眾愕然，莫知何是。大師曰：「大眾，大眾作意聽！世人自色身是城，眼耳鼻舌身即是城門，外有六門，內有意門。心即是地，性即是王，性在王在，性去王無，性在身心存，性去身壞。佛是自性作，莫向身外[80]求。自性迷，佛即眾生；自性悟，眾

---

[71] 原作「只為下根，說近說遠，只緣上智」。

[72] 原作「不名」。

[73] 原作「言佛」。

[74] 原缺「人」字。

[75] 原缺「人」字。

[76] 原作「西」。

[77] 原缺「十」字。

[78] 原作「問」。

[79] 原作「曰」。

[80] 原缺「外」字。

生即是佛。慈悲即是觀音,喜捨名為勢至,能淨是釋迦,平直[81]是彌勒,人我是須彌,邪心是大海,煩惱是波浪,毒心是惡龍,塵勞是魚鼈,虛妄即是神鬼,三毒即是地獄,愚癡即是畜生,十善是天堂。無人我[82],須彌自倒;除邪心,海水竭;煩惱無,波浪滅;毒害除,魚龍絕。自心地上,覺性如來,施大智慧,光明照曜,六門清淨,照破[83]六欲諸天。下照三毒若除,地獄一時消滅,內外明徹,不異西方,不作此修,如何到彼?」

座下聞[84]說,讚聲徹天,應是迷人,了[85]然便見。使君禮拜,讚言:「善哉!善哉!普願法界眾生,聞者一時悟解。」大師言:「善知識,若欲修行,在家亦得,不由在寺。在寺不修,如西方心惡之人,在家若修行,如東方人修善。但願自家修清淨,即是西[86]方。」

---

81 原作「真」。

82 原作「我無人」。

83 原作「波」。

84 原作「問」。

85 原作「人」。

86 原作「惡」。

問題討論：

1. 請問惠能在中國禪宗史中，扮演了一個怎樣的角色和地位？

2. 閱讀了《壇經》文本之後，請問你認為惠能禪學，其最重要的本質、內涵、特點為何？

3. 一般認為，禪宗是不立文字，不看重經典的，請問，這樣的思想，是否符合能禪學的本意呢？

4.《壇經》的版本，在歷史上經過多次的改寫、改造，請問你，我們在選擇《壇經》版本時，應注意哪些問題。

延伸閱讀：

1. 印順，《中國禪宗史》，臺北，正聞出版社，1992 年。

2. 柳田聖山撰，吳汝鈞譯，《中國禪思想史》，臺北，商務印書館，1992 年。

3. 洪修平，《中國禪學思想史》，臺北，文津出版社，1994 年。

4. 張國一，《唐代禪宗心性思想》，臺北，法鼓文化，2004 年。

5. 楊惠南，《惠能》，臺北，東大圖書，1993 年。

6. 傅偉勳，〈《壇經》惠能頓悟禪教深層義蘊試探〉，《中國哲學史研究》，1989 年，第 3 期。

7. 聖嚴，〈六祖壇經的思想〉，《中華佛學學報》第 3 期，1990 年 4 月。

8. 張國一，〈歷代文獻中的慧能心性思探究〉，《圓光佛學學報》，第 5 期，2000 年 12 月，頁 89-117。

十八、臨濟義玄經典選讀

張 國一

單元旨要：

中國禪宗，大盛於六祖惠能。其下，「一花開五葉，結果自然成」，禪之發達，盛極熱烈，「五葉」，即為仰宗、臨濟宗、曹洞宗、雲門宗、法眼宗。臨濟義玄 (866 卒)，即臨濟宗的創始者。

臨濟禪，特重發揮「性在作用」禪法。一個解脫的禪者，日常言語，舉手投足，無非皆他佛性之展現！想知道佛「性」是什麼嗎？禪者揮一揮手、踢一腳，乃至打學生一拳，就「在」他這些身心「作用」中！

這樣的新禪法，比起達磨以來，看重經教的禪風，[1] 大大邁進了一步。說佛，說道，不必依賴佛典，就在我禪者言語動止當中，這，就是佛，就是道！禪，大略自此，[2] 竟走入一個離經超教，喝佛罵祖，所謂機鋒棒喝，大機大用的新時代！

當然，這並不表示，禪，必反對經教！學人讀經，有助悟道，無妨令讀之 (像達磨、惠能教人那樣)；若執著經義，落文字障，正可施棒施喝，令反本歸源了！「性在作用」，為禪門發展出來一種新方便，並非唯一

---

[1] 達磨乃至五祖弘忍，看重《楞伽經》，六祖惠能則看重《金剛經》，都是看重借經教傳禪的。

[2] 當然，此一禪風，並非創自臨濟義玄，而是他的師祖馬祖道一所開啟的。

的接眾方法，這是讀者應加注意的！

這樣的新禪風，現代學者已指出，或更接近佛陀本懷！[3] 佛陀原初說法，亦無經典可依據的，借言教、身教，導學人以悟入。「性在作用」，為對佛陀「身教」之繼承與發揮！身教，往往影響力更甚於言教，學人孺慕、浸潤既久，有助引導其開悟，是無可疑義的。

當然，此一新禪風，後世落入不具格、道眼未明的瞎盲禪師手中，成狂禪一流，弄眉擠眼，做模做樣，自誤誤人！還不如依循經教，老老實實，聞思修道了。

臨濟禪，發揚「性在作用」，對中國禪門的影響，為無與倫比的。「言教」的禪，推廣成「身教」的禪，禪，他原始更為豐富、活潑的內涵，被揭示出來了。靜態的教學，轉為動態的教學，禪門，一時間，活潑熱烈極了！

臨濟禪，大略，得到了中國禪門最高的肯定與尊崇，後世中國（乃至日本、韓國）叢林，無非皆臨濟兒孫了！（另一支興盛的宗派為曹洞宗。）

今天，我們要探究臨濟義玄的生平、思想，很可惜，欠缺他在世時，即編寫完成的一手文獻可供參考。最早收錄臨濟資料的後代燈史，為《祖堂集》(952)、《景德傳燈錄》(1004)，與《天聖廣燈錄》(1029)。這是我們今天，探究臨濟義玄，較早、較可信賴的三種資料。[4]

---

[3] 可參印順：《中國禪宗史》。

[4] 研究臨濟義玄，可供參考較完備的後代燈史資料，約共 24 種。可參張國一：《唐代禪宗心性思想》，頁 169-172。

　　本文，即選取了《祖堂集》卷 19 之「臨濟和尚」（全文）、《景德傳燈錄》卷 28 之「鎮州臨濟義玄和尚」（節選）、《天聖廣燈錄》卷 11 之「鎮州臨濟院義玄慧照禪師」（節選）三段文字。[5] 其中錄有臨濟生平簡史，也有他比較清楚，具理論性的，生動活潑的開禪說法。透過三種資料，我們可以對臨濟義玄，得到一個較可信賴、深入的理解了。

　　臨濟禪，當然，一般是專接利根學人的！搖一搖手，推一下，打一掌，一般學人，大略不受用的。若又掉落其中尋思，真要如丈二金剛，摸不著腦袋了！

---

　　[5]　《景德傳燈錄》卷 12 與《天聖廣燈錄》卷 10，另尚收錄有臨濟與學生之間的機鋒問答，較欠缺理論性，本文暫不錄之，讀者可自行參閱。

選讀文本：

1.《祖堂集》之「臨濟和尚」（全文）

　　臨濟和尚，嗣黃蘗，在鎮州，師諱義玄，姓刑，曹南人也，自契黃蘗鋒機，乃闡化於河北，提綱峻速，示教幽深。其餘樞祕難陳，示誨略申少分。

　　黃蘗和尚告眾曰：「於昔時同參大寂道友，名曰大愚，此人諸方行腳，法眼明微，今在高安，願不好群居，猶栖山舍。與余相別時，叮囑云：『他後或逢靈利[6]者，指一人來相訪。』」

　　于時師在眾，聞已，便往造謁，既到其所，據陳上說。至夜間，於大愚前說《瑜伽論》，譚[7]唯識，附申問難。大愚畢夕峭然不對，及至旦來，謂師曰：「老僧獨居山舍，念子遠來，且延一宿，何故夜間於吾前無羞慚，放不淨？」言訖，杖之數下，推出，關卻門。

　　師回黃蘗，復陳上說，黃蘗聞已，稽首曰：「作者如猛火然，喜子遇人，何乃虛往？」

　　師又去，復見大愚，大愚曰：「前時無慚愧，今日何故又來？」言訖便棒，推出門。

---

[6]　按，應即「伶俐」。

[7]　即「談」也。

師復返黃蘗：「啟聞和尚，此迴再返，不是空歸。」黃蘗曰：「何故如此？」師曰：「於一棒下入佛境界，假使百劫粉骨碎身，頂擎遶須彌山經無量帀，報此深恩，莫可酬得。」黃蘗聞已，喜之異常曰：「子且解歇，更自出身。」

師過旬日，又辭黃蘗，至大愚所。大愚纔見，便擬棒師，師接得棒子，便抱倒大愚，乃就其背毆之數拳，大愚遂連點頭曰：「吾獨居山舍，將謂空過一生，不期今日卻得一子。」

大愚臨遷化時，囑師云：「子自不負平生，又乃終吾一世，已後出世傳心，第一莫忘黃蘗。」自後，師於鎮府匡化，雖承黃蘗，常讚大愚。至於化門，多行棒喝。

有時謂眾云：「但一切時中更莫間斷，觸目皆是，因何不會？只為情生智隔，想變體殊，所以三界輪迴，受種種苦。大德，心法無形，通貫十方，在眼曰見，在耳曰聞，在手執捉，在腳雲奔。本是一精明，分成六和合。心若不生，隨處解脫。大德，欲得山僧見處，坐斷報化佛頭。十地滿心，猶如客作兒，何以如此？蓋為不達三祇劫空，所以有此障。若是真正道流，盡不如此。大德，山僧略為諸人大約話破綱宗，切須自看，可惜時光，各自努力。」

2.《景德傳燈錄》之「鎮州臨濟義玄和尚」（節選）

鎮州臨濟義玄和尚示眾曰：「今時學人，且要明取自己真正見解。若得自己見解，即不被生死染，去住自由，不要求他殊勝，殊勝自備。如今道流，且要不滯於惑，要用便用。」

「如今不得，病在何處？病在不自信處。自信不及，即便忙忙[8]，徇一切境。大德[9]，若能歇得念念馳求心，便與祖師不別。汝欲識祖師麼？即汝目前聽法底是，學人信不及，便向外馳求。得者只是文字學，與他祖師大遠在。」

「莫錯！大德，此時不遇，萬劫千生，輪迴三界，徇好惡境，向驢牛肚裏去也。如今諸人，與古聖何別？汝且欠少什麼？六道神光，未曾間歇，若能如此見，是一生無事人。一念淨光，是汝屋裏法身佛；一念無分別光，是汝報身佛；一念無差別光，是汝化身佛。」

「此三身，即是今日目前聽法底人，為不向外求，有此三種功用，據教三種名為極則。約山僧道，三種是名言，故云：身依義而立，土據體而論。法性身、法性土，明知是光影，大德，且要識取弄光影人，是諸佛本源，是一切道流歸舍處。」

「大德，四大身，不解說法聽法，虛空，不解說法聽法。是汝目前歷歷孤明，勿形段者，解說法聽法。所以山僧向汝道：五蘊身田內，有無位真人，堂堂顯露，無絲髮許間隔，何不識取！」

「心法無形，通貫十方，在眼曰見，在耳曰聞，在手執捉，在足運奔，心若不在，隨處解脫。山僧見處，坐斷報化佛頂[10]，十地滿心，猶如客作兒，等妙二覺，如擔枷帶鎖，羅漢辟支，猶如糞土，菩提涅槃，繫驢馬橛。何以如斯？蓋為不達三祇劫空，有此障隔，若是真道流，

8　應為「茫茫」。

9　原作「脫大德」。

10　應為「頭」。

盡不如此。如今略為諸人，大約話破，自看遠近，時光可惜，各自努力，珍重！」

3.《天聖廣燈錄》之「鎮州臨濟院義玄慧照禪師」（節選）

「道流，儞祇有一箇父母，更求何物？儞自返照看。古人云：演若達多失却頭，求心歇處即無事。大德，且要平常，莫作模樣。有一般不識好惡秀[11]兵，便即見神見鬼，指東畫西，好晴好雨。如是之流，盡須抵債，向閻老前，吞熱鐵丸有日。好人家男女，被者一般野狐精魅所著，便即捏怪，瞎屢生，索飯錢有日在。」

師又云：「佛法無用功處，祇是平常無事，屙屎送尿，著衣喫飯，困來即臥，愚人笑我，智乃知焉。古人云：向外作功夫，總是癡頑漢。儞且隨處作主，立處皆真，境來迴換不得。縱有從來習氣，五無間業，自為解脫大海。」

問：「如何是佛魔？」師云：「儞一念心疑處，是佛魔，儞若達得萬法無生，心如幻化，更無一塵一法，處處清淨是佛。然佛與魔是染淨二境，約山僧見處，無佛無眾生，無古無今，得者便得，不歷時節，無修無證，無得無失，一切時中，更無別法，設有一法過此者，我說如夢如化。山僧所說，皆是道流即今目前，孤明歷歷地聽者。此人處處不滯，通貫十方三界，自在入一切境差別，不能迴換。一剎那間，透入法界，逢佛說佛，逢祖說祖，逢羅漢說羅漢，逢餓鬼說餓鬼，向一切處，遊履國土，教化眾生，未曾離一念。隨處清淨，光透十方，萬法一如。」

---

11 或為「禿」。

　　師云：「儞但一切入凡入聖，入染入淨，入諸佛國土，入彌勒樓閣，入毗盧遮那法界，處處皆現國土成住壞空。佛出于世，轉大法輪，即入涅槃，不見有去來相貌，求其生死，了不可得。便入無生法界，處處遊履國土，入華藏世界，盡見諸法空相，皆無實法，唯有聽法無依道人，是諸佛之母。所以佛從無依生，若悟無依，佛亦無得，若如是見得者，是真正見解。學人不了，為執名句，被他凡聖名礙，所以障其道眼，不得分明。祇如十二分教，皆是表顯之說，學者不會，便向表顯名句上生解，皆是依倚，落在因果，未免三界生死。儞若欲得生死、去住、脫著自由，即今識取聽法底人，無形無相，無根無本，無住處，活撥撥[12]地，應是萬種施設用處，祇是無處。所覓著轉遠，求之轉乖，號之為祕密。」

　　「一切諸天、神仙、阿修羅、大力鬼，亦有神通，應是佛否？道流莫錯，祇如阿修羅與天帝釋戰，戰敗，領八萬四千眷屬，入藕絲孔中藏，莫是聖否？如山僧所舉，皆是業通、依通。夫如佛六通者不然，入色界，不被色惑，入聲界，不被聲惑，入香界，不被香惑，入味界，不被味惑，入觸界，不被觸惑，入法界，不被法惑。所以達六種色聲香味觸法，皆是空相，不能繫縛。此無依道人，雖是五蘊漏質，便是地行神通。」

　　「十方諸佛現前，無一念心喜；三塗地獄頓現，無一念心怖。緣何如此？我見諸法空相，變即有，不變師[13]無。三界唯心，萬法唯識，所以夢幻空花，何勞把捉。唯有道流目前現令[14]聽法底人，入火不燒，

---

[12]　應為「潑」。

[13]　按，應為「即」。

[14]　按，應為「今」。

入水不溺，入三塗地獄如遊園觀，入餓鬼畜生而不受報。緣何如此？無嫌底法，儞若愛聖憎凡，生死海裏浮沈。煩惱由心故有，無心，煩惱何拘，不勞分別取相，自然得道須臾。儞擬傍家波波地學得，於三祇劫中，終歸生死，不如無事，向叢林中，牀角頭，交脚坐。」

「大德，儞莫認衣，衣不能動，人能著衣。有簡清淨衣，有簡無生衣、菩提衣、涅槃衣，有祖衣、有佛衣，大德，但有聲名文句，皆悉是衣變。從臍輪氣海中鼓激，牙齒敲磕，成其句義，明知是幻化。大德，外發聲語業，內表心所法，以思有念，皆悉是衣。儞祇麼認他著底衣為實解，縱經塵劫，祇是衣通，三界循還，輪迴生死，不如無事。」

師云：「為儞向一切處馳求，心不能歇，所以祖師言：咄哉！丈夫，將頭覓頭。儞言下便自迴光返照，更不別求，知身心與祖佛不別，當下無事，方名得法。大德，山僧今時，事不獲已，話度說出許多不才淨，儞且莫錯，據我見處，實無許多般道理，要用便用，不用便休。」

師云：「見因緣空、心空、法空，一念決定，迥然無事，便是焚燒經像。大德，若如是達得，免被他凡聖名礙，為儞祇向空拳、指上生實解，根境法中虛捏怪，自輕而退屈，言我是凡夫，他是聖人。禿屢生，有甚死急？披他師子皮，却作野干鳴。大丈夫漢，不作丈夫氣息，自家屋裏物不肯信，祇麼向外覓，上他古人閒名句，倚陰博陽，不能持達，逢境便緣，逢塵便執，觸處惑起，自無準定。」

問題討論：

1. 請問惠能以後，「一花開五葉」，「五葉」是指哪五個宗派？

2. 根據臨濟義玄的文獻與說理，請問他所說的佛性的內涵為何？

3. 臨濟義玄，與達磨、惠能所說的佛性內涵，同異為何？請試做一分析比較。

4. 請問什麼是「性在作用」禪法？他的原理、內涵為何？

5. 請問是否有臨濟義玄一手文獻傳世？今天探究臨濟義玄，哪些後代燈史，是較早、較可信賴的？

延伸閱讀：

1. 印順，《中國禪宗史》，臺北，正聞出版社，1992 年。

2. 柳田聖山撰，吳汝鈞譯，《中國禪思想史》，臺北，商務印書館，1992 年。

3. 洪修平，《中國禪學思想史》，臺北，文津出版社，1994 年。

4. 張國一，《唐代禪宗心性思想》，臺北，法鼓文化，2004 年。

5. 金起賢，〈從臨濟義玄之禪思想看中國禪宗哲學之諸特性〉，《中國文化月刊》，第 178 期，1994 年 8 月。

6. 吳汝鈞，〈臨濟禪〉，《獅子吼》，第 33 卷第 6 期，1994 年 6 月。

7. 張國一，〈臨濟義玄的心性思想〉，《海潮音》，第 84 卷第 7、8、9、10 期，2003 年 7 月、8 月、9 月、10 月。

叢書編號 AA003　　　　　　　978-986-5608-08-8

哲學經典選讀

著　　者	王志銘、王靈康、徐佐銘、張國一、鄭鈞瑋、蘇富芝
主　　編	王靈康
內文排版	中茂分色製版印刷事業股份有限公司
封面設計	廖雪雅
發 行 人	張家宜
社　　長	林信成
總 編 輯	吳秋霞
行政編輯	張瑜倫
行銷企劃	陳卉綺
出　　版	淡江大學出版中心
	地址：25137 新北市淡水區英專路151號
	電話：02-86318661/傳真：02-86318660
總 經 銷	紅螞蟻圖書有限公司
	地址：台北市114內湖區舊宗路2段121巷19號
	電話：02-27953656/傳真：02-27954100

出版日期　　2016年9月 一版一刷

定　　價　　300元

國家圖書館出版品預行編目資料

哲學經典選讀 / 王志銘等編著. -- 一版. -- 新北市
: 淡大出版中心, 2016.03
　　面；　公分
ISBN 978-986-5608-08-8(平裝)
1.哲學 2.文集
107　　　　　　　　　　　　105001791